IT'S ALL ABOUT JESUS

IT'S ALL ABOUT JESUS

A Book of Devotional Readings
—to be read *by* older children
—to be read *to* young children

ALLAN HART JAHSMANN

Illustrations by Art Kirchhoff

Publishing House
St. Louis   London

Library of Congress Cataloging in Publication Data
Jahsmann, Allan Hart.
    It's all about Jesus.

    SUMMARY: Stories from the life of Jesus with supplemental devotions for each.
    1. Jesus Christ — Biography — Juvenile literature. 2. Children — Prayer-books and
devotions — English — 1961-   [1. Jesus Christ — Biography. 2. Prayer books and
devotions] I. Kirchhoff, Art, ill. II. Title.
BT302.J25   232.9   74-21233
ISBN 0-570-03025-0
ISBN 0-570-03031-5 pbk.

Concordia Publishing House, St. Louis, Missouri
Concordia Publishing House Ltd., London, E. C. 1
Copyright © 1975 Concordia Publishing House

MANUFACTURED IN THE UNITED STATES OF AMERICA

Jesus called a child to Him, put His arms around him, and said to His followers, "The person who welcomes a child in My name welcomes Me; and whoever welcomes Me, welcomes not only Me but also the one who sent Me."

Mark 9:37

*This book is dedicated
to the glory of Jesus,
who loves every child
on earth.*

Contents

Let Me Introduce the Book to You

This is a book about Jesus. You probably know a little about Him — or maybe even quite a bit. You know how He was born in a little town called Bethlehem in the country called Palestine.

Every Christmas you hear songs and stories of wonderful things that happened when Jesus was born. That night, above the fields near Bethlehem, angels appeared and told shepherds, who were watching their sheep, that their Savior, Christ the Lord, had been born.

Then a great big choir of angels appeared with them in the sky. "Glory to God in the highest and on earth peace," they sang. When they went away, the shepherds hurried off and found the baby lying in a manger.

Other wonderful things happened right before and after Jesus was born. They were all God's way of telling us that this Child Jesus was no ordinary person. He was the Son of God. He would be the Light of the world and would save God's people from their sins.

There's a lot more to know about Jesus and a lot to be learned from Him. That's why I wrote these readings about Him.

I hope you'll read and think and talk about them. They'll help you know Jesus better and show you how to live with Him wherever you are and forever. That's worth knowing!

ALLAN HART JAHSMANN

The Time Jesus Stayed at His Church

Jesus grew up in a town called Nazareth in that part of Palestine called Galilee. The Bible says, "As the Boy grew, He became big and strong and full of wisdom."

Every year Jesus' parents went from Nazareth to Jerusalem for the Passover festival, a reminder of how God saved the Israelites from slavery in Egypt. Most Jewish people still celebrate it every year wherever they are.

When Jesus was 12, they all went again for the Passover festival. It was always an exciting trip to the big city, but for Jesus there was a special excitement, as we shall see.

After several days, when the celebration was over, Mary and Joseph started home with a lot of other people from Nazareth. But Jesus stayed in Jerusalem without His parents knowing it. They thought He was with His friends somewhere in the crowd.

After traveling all day, Mary and Joseph started looking for their Son. When they couldn't find Him, they hurried back to Jerusalem and began looking everywhere in the big city. They searched for several days.

Finally on the third day, Mary and Joseph found Jesus in the temple. He was sitting with teachers, listening to them and asking them questions. They were amazed at

what a boy knew about God and books written by prophets.

At first Jesus' mother was angry with Him for staying at church. "Son, why did You worry us? Your father and I have been trying to find You," she said.

"Why did you have to look for Me? Didn't you know I would be in My Father's house?" Jesus replied.

They didn't know what to say to that, but they asked Jesus to return home with them, and He obeyed. He went back with them to Nazareth. There He grew bigger and wiser, and in ways that pleased God and people.

Something more to think about: Jesus grew up with the blessings of God. What were some of these blessings?

How did He receive them? Already as a boy, Jesus thought of God as His Father. He also began to realize that He was the Son of God. When we realize that God is our Father and that we are His children, what will we want to do as we get older?

Words to help us pray: Dear Jesus, You knew and loved God already when You were a boy. Give us Your Holy Spirit so that we will enjoy going to God's house the way You did. Amen.

How the Devil Tried to Spoil Jesus

Jesus began His work of preaching and teaching when He was 30 years old. Before that He had been a carpenter in Nazareth.

When Jesus was about to begin His ministry, the devil tried to spoil Him and what He planned to do for God. Here is the story of how the devil tempted Jesus.

Soon after His baptism Jesus went into a lonely part of His country to think about what God wanted Him to do for the world. For 40 days Jesus lived there in the desert. During that time He hardly ate anything.

When Jesus was very hungry, the devil came to Him and said: "If You really are the Son of God, order these stones to turn into bread." But Jesus answered: "It is written, 'A man can't live just on bread. But he can live by every word that God speaks.' " You see, being true to God is far more important than having bread and other things.

Then the devil took Jesus to the highest part of the temple in Jerusalem, where he said to Him: "If you want people to believe You are God's Son, jump off. The Bible says, 'God will make His angels take care of you. They will catch you, and not even your toe will get hurt on the stones below.' "

The devil used words from the Bible to tempt Jesus to show off and do something foolish. But Jesus said: "You must not test the Lord, your God."

Then the devil took Jesus to a high mountain and pictured for Him all the rich and great places of the world. There he said to Jesus: "If you'll kneel down and worship me, I will give You all this power and glory." But Jesus answered: "Go away, Satan! The Bible says, 'You are to worship the Lord. He is your God. Serve only Him!'" Then the devil left Jesus.

Something more to think about: Almost everyone, Christian or not, believes there are a devil and other evil spirits in the world. And there are. What might tempt us to choose money and things and give up living according to God's Word and ways? How are we sometimes tempted to show off and become important? Why do we sometimes wish to be rich and powerful? What's wrong with that?

Words to help us pray: Our Father in heaven, never let the devil tempt us. Please get us out of all evil. Give us the Spirit of Jesus so that we, too, will live in Your kingdom with Jesus forever. Amen.

Why Jesus Chose Some Partners

Long before Jesus lived on earth, the prophet Isaiah wrote: "The people who live in darkness will see a great Light. The Light will shine on those who live in the dark land of death."

When Jesus came back from being alone in the desert

for 40 days and 40 nights, He quit His carpenter work in Nazareth. He was that Light the prophet Isaiah had said would come, and He had other work to do. Jesus began to travel, and wherever He went He told people, "Turn away from your sins because the kingdom of heaven is near."

One day Jesus was preaching on the shore of a lake called the Sea of Galilee. A big crowd gathered to hear Him speak the Word of God, and many people began to push their way closer to Him.

On the beach were two boats. The fishermen who owned them were washing their nets nearby. Jesus got into one of the boats, which belonged to a man named Simon. Jesus had met Simon not long before and had given Simon the extra name "Peter."

"Take your boat out a little way from the shore," Jesus said to Simon Peter. Then Jesus taught the crowd from the boat.

When He had finished speaking, Jesus said, "Now row the boat out further to the deep water, and let down your nets for a catch."

"We worked all night long and caught nothing," replied Simon Peter. "But if You say so, I will let down the nets."

So Peter and his helpers rowed out to the deep water. As soon as they dropped the nets into the water, fish swam into them—so many fish that the nets began to tear.

Simon Peter and his helpers called to their partners to come with the other boat and help them. The men filled both boats so full of fish that they almost sank.

When Simon Peter saw what had happened, he knelt down in front of Jesus and said, "Go away from me, Lord! I am a sinful man!"

But Jesus said to Simon, "Don't be afraid. From now on you will be catching people." Jesus meant that Peter and his partners James and John would be helping Him bring people into God's kingdom and church.

After Simon Peter and his partners had brought their boats back to the beach, they left everything behind them and went with Jesus.

Something more to think about: How is Jesus still the Light of the world? What is the way into heaven that

He shows people? Simon Peter and his brother Andrew had met Jesus at least once before. How did Peter show faith in Jesus? Why did Peter become afraid of Jesus when he saw all the fish? What did Jesus want Peter and his partners to do from then on? How can we be partners with Jesus?

Words to help us pray and do: Lord Jesus, Light of the world, give us the faith but not the fear that Simon Peter had when he saw Your power. Make us glad to help You in Your work of bringing people into the kingdom of heaven. Amen.

A Time When Jesus Got Very Angry

Not long after Jesus chose some men to be His partners, He went with them to Jerusalem. The time had come to celebrate the Passover. Jews from all over the world came to Jerusalem for the festival in the big, beautiful temple.

When Jesus and His disciples entered the temple yard, He was shocked at what He saw. The place looked and sounded like a cattle market. It was filled with men selling cows and sheep and pigeons to people who needed sacrifices.

The merchants shouted to the customers. Money traders, sitting at tables inside the temple yard, exchanged

Jewish money for the money people brought from other countries.

All of this business and noise inside the temple court-yard made Jesus very angry. He made a whip out of some ropes He found and drove the sheep and cattle and their owners off the temple grounds. Then He tipped over the tables of the money traders. Their coins went flying. And He said to the men selling pigeons, "Get them out of here! Don't you dare make My Father's house a store!"

No one tried to stop Jesus. The traders knew they were wrong, so away they ran, catching as much of what they owned as they could. When Jesus' disciples saw what He had done, they remembered that their Bible said, "The love of God's house will burn like a fire in the Savior of God's people."

The news of what Jesus had done at the temple spread quickly. When the rulers of the temple heard the reports, they came and asked Jesus, "What miracle can You perform to prove You had the right to chase out the traders?"

"Tear down this temple, and in 3 days I will build it again," Jesus answered.

The Jewish leaders thought Jesus was talking about the temple building. So they said: "It has taken 46 years to build this temple. You think You could build it again in 3 days?" But the temple Jesus meant was His body. Later when Jesus rose from death on the third day, His disciples remembered what He had said.

Something more to think about: In the Old Testament God commanded His people to sacrifice animals and birds.

So what made Jesus angry? What did Jesus show by His actions? Why was it dangerous for Jesus to do what He did? Why don't we ever have to be afraid to do what we know is right?

Words to help us pray: Lord Jesus, You weren't afraid to risk Your life for God, Your Father. Increase Your Holy Spirit in us. Then we will not be afraid to serve You. Amen.

Water for Your Spirit

On a trip back to Galilee from Jerusalem, Jesus went through Samaria. Almost in the center of Samaria was the little city of Sychar. Near it, out in a field, was a famous well called Jacob's Well.

That day Jesus was tired and hungry. So He sat down by the well while His disciples went to town to buy some food.

"Give Me a drink of water," Jesus said to a woman who had come from the town to get water out of the well. This surprised her. "You are a Jew and I am a Samaritan. How could You ask me for a drink?" she said. Most Jews thought they were better than the people of Samaria.

"If you knew what God gives and who I am," Jesus said, "you would ask Me for living water. Everyone who drinks the water in this well will get thirsty soon again. But whoever drinks the water I give will never be thirsty."

The woman said, "Sir, give me that water. Then I will not have to keep coming here." You see, she didn't understand. She thought Jesus was still talking about well water. But Jesus meant water for her spirit. He was giving people the good news about God.

Then Jesus began to give her that Good News. He said, "Go and get your husband." "I don't have a husband," she replied. "I know. You sin by living with many men," Jesus told her. This made her talk to Jesus about how to be saved.

Finally Jesus said, "I am the Christ, the Messiah, the Savior who was to come." When the woman heard this, she became very excited. Off she ran to the town. And she even forgot her jar at the well. "Come and see a man who told me everything I've ever done," she said to people in the town. "Could He be the Messiah?" she asked.

The woman believed what Jesus said and so did many others when they heard her. So they all hurried out to the well and begged Jesus to stay with them. He and His disciples stayed for 2 days. When they left the town, people said to the woman, "Now we know that He really is the Savior of the world."

Something more to think about: Why was Jesus willing to talk to anybody? Why are some people not willing to have anything to do with people from another country or race? What is the living water that God gives to anyone who wants it? How does He give it? How can we have Jesus staying with us all the time?

Words to help us pray: Dear Jesus, thank You for giving us water for our spirit. Your love is an ocean of fresh water. Please stay with us in our home and never leave us. Amen.

A Sick Man's Best Friend

Near one of the city gates of Jerusalem there was a pool called Bethesda, which means "house of mercy." Around it someone had built five porches as shelters for the sick people who stayed there.

The sick, lame, and blind people lying by the pool hoped to be cured because from time to time an angel caused a spring in the pool to bubble. While it bubbled, the first person who got in became well.

One of the people waiting to be cured was a man who had been lying there 38 years. Week after week, month after month, year after year, he hoped to get into the water first, but never could.

One day Jesus came to this hospital by the pool. He

saw the man who had been sick so long and said to him, "Do you want to get well?"

The man answered sadly, "Sir, I don't have anyone to put me into the pool when the water bubbles up. While I am dragging myself to the water, someone else gets there first."

"Get up, take your mat, and walk," Jesus said to him. When the man heard these words, he immediately got well, picked up his mat, and began walking. How excited he must have been!

But this happened on a Sabbath day, and in those times the Jews weren't to do anything on the Sabbath. So when the rulers saw the man carrying his mat, they stopped him and said, "This is a Sabbath. It is against the law for you to be carrying your mat."

The healed man said, "The man who made me well told me to pick up my mat and walk." When the officers asked, "Who told you to do that?" the man couldn't tell them.

A little later Jesus saw the man in the temple. He said to him, "Now that you are well, quit sinning or something worse may happen to you." Then the man went and told the officers that Jesus had healed him.

So they went and talked to Jesus about what He had done. "My Father works all the time, and I too must work," Jesus told them. This made them very angry, and they decided to kill Jesus. He had broken their Sabbath law. He had said God was His Father and He was like God.

Something more to think about: Why didn't Jesus worry about breaking the Sabbath law? What's wrong when people think that keeping laws is more important than helping people? Why did the leaders of the Jews decide to kill Jesus? If you ever said you were like God when you do what He does, how might people feel about you?

Words to help us pray and do: Dear Jesus, Friend of all who are sick and waiting to be healed, may we never forget that, like Your Father, You always help us in our sickness or trouble. Make us willing to help others whenever we can. We ask it for Your name's sake. Amen.

The Way Jesus Wants Us to Pray

"When you pray, don't use a lot of words like the people do who think God will hear them because their prayers are long. Your Father in heaven already knows what you need before you ask Him," Jesus told his disciples. Then He gave them a short prayer as an example of how they should pray. It's called the Lord's Prayer.

"When you pray," said Jesus, "say: Our Father in heaven." Jesus was telling us that we can speak to God as children speak to a loving father. God's children want their Father's name to be honored and kept holy. So Jesus told us to pray, "Hallowed be Your name."

Jesus wants God to rule all people with His love. He wants the whole world to have life with God. That's why He asks us to pray, "May Your kingdom come."

The next example Jesus gave was, "Your will be done on earth as it is in heaven." People who really love God want to do His will. And they want God's will to be done on earth the way it is done by His angels in heaven.

Then Jesus gave some examples of other prayers. By praying "Give us this day our daily bread," we ask God for whatever we need each day.

"And forgive us our trespasses [the sins we have done], as we forgive those who trespass against us." When we forgive what others do to us, we show we believe that God forgives us too.

Finally, Jesus told us to say, "And lead us not into temptation, but deliver us from evil." We know that the devil tempts people. Sometimes God lets him do it to test our love and make it stronger. But in this last petition of His model prayer we ask God to save us from the devil's temptations.

Something more to think about: Some people think it does them some good just to say the words of the Lord's Prayer. What do they forget Jesus said about praying? We often say the sample prayer Jesus gave us because it's such a perfect prayer. But only *when* do we really pray it?

Another way to say the Lord's Prayer: Our Father in heaven, holy be Your name. Your kingdom come. Your

will be done on earth as in heaven. Give us today our
daily bread. Forgive us our sins as we forgive those who
sin against us. Do not bring us to the test, but deliver us
from evil. For the kingdom, the power, and the glory are
Yours now and forever.

A Soldier Who Believed in Jesus

When Jesus was a young man, He lived in the city of
Capernaum. A Roman army officer with over 100 soldiers
also lived there, because the Romans were ruling the Jews.

Even though most Jews hated the Romans, the Roman captain felt very friendly toward the Jews in his town. He even built a synagogue (a church and school) for them. So even before the Roman officer met Jesus, he must have had some faith in the God the Jews worshiped.

This Roman officer had a servant who probably had worked for him a long time and was dear to him. But now the servant was very sick and was about to die.

When the Roman captain heard that Jesus was back in Capernaum, he asked the town's leaders to beg Jesus to heal his servant. He knew Jesus had healed other sick people. The leaders went to Jesus and said, "The Roman captain loves our people. He even built a synagogue for us. Please go and heal his servant, whom he loves very much."

So Jesus went with the men. But as He approached the house where the officer and his servant lived, the captain sent some friends out to Jesus with a message: "Sir, I don't deserve to have You come into my house."

The Roman officer believed that Jesus was the Son of God, who didn't have to come into his house. "Just give the order and my servant will get well," he said. "I get my power from officers above me, and I have soldiers under me. If I tell my servants to do something, they do it," he added. The officer was sure that Jesus could do the same.

Jesus was surprised when He heard what the Roman captain believed. He said to the people with Him, "I have never seen such faith as this in anyone in Israel." Then He said to the officer's friends, "Go; what the captain believes will be done for him." When the messengers went back to the captain's house, they found his servant well.

Something more to think about: If someone asked you to pray to Jesus for him, what could you say about his faith? Why do people sometimes ask Christians to pray for others? How is Jesus able to help people who don't even know Him? What made the officer's faith in Jesus great? How great do you think your faith is?

A prayer for greater faith: Savior and Helper of all people, give us faith like the Roman officer had. And make us as concerned about the welfare of others as he was. For Your name's sake we ask it. Amen.

The Best Gift You'll Ever Get

One day Jesus was teaching a houseful of Bible students, called scribes, who had come from all over Galilee and Judea.

Just then four men came down the street carrying on a mattress a man who couldn't walk. They were bringing him to Jesus because they believed Jesus could heal him.

When they saw they couldn't get into the house, they carried their friend up to the flat roof. Opening it up, they let him down on his bed right in front of Jesus.

When Jesus saw how much faith the four men had, He

said to the crippled man, "Son, be happy; your sins are forgiven." Jesus wanted everyone in the house to know that sin is the most serious sickness.

The words made the sick man very happy. He had been afraid that the great Teacher, the one people were saying was the Son of God, would not be kind to him. But the scribes thought to themselves: "No man can forgive sins; only God can! This man is saying He can do what only God can do."

Jesus knew what the men around Him were thinking. So He asked them, "Is it easier to say, 'Your sins are forgiven,' or to say, 'Get up and walk'?" Jesus was pointing out that for an ordinary man both are impossible. But before they could answer, Jesus said: "I will prove to you that I have the power to forgive sins."

Then Jesus said to the man on the bed, "Get up. Pick up your bedroll and go home!" Right away the sick man became well and strong. Praising God, he picked up the mat he had been lying on and started for home. When the people in the house saw what Jesus had done, they were all amazed. They said, "What a wonderful thing we have seen today!"

The best and most important gift anyone can get from God is the forgiveness of sins. But God can also heal all our sicknesses and troubles. And He often does.

Something more to think about: How did Jesus show that forgiveness is God's best gift? What didn't the men who were attending Jesus' school believe? Why not? How did Jesus prove that He had the power to forgive sins?

People sometimes say, "If you've got your health, you've got just about everything." What do they mean by that? Why is the forgiveness and love of God worth much more than health? How can we always have God's love?

Words to help us praise God: Lord God, our Father in heaven, we praise and thank You for the best of all the gifts You give people through Your son, Jesus, our Savior. We are happy that in Your kingdom we can always be sure of Your love and help. Amen.

What to Do in a Bad Storm

Once, at the end of a busy day, Jesus decided to get away from the crowds that were following Him. He stepped into a ship someone let Him use. Then He said to His disciples, "Let's go over to the other side of the lake." So off they went.

The lake was calm and quiet. A soft, warm breeze was blowing over the water. And Jesus was very tired. He lay down at one end of the ship and soon was fast asleep.

Suddenly a storm hit the lake. Huge waves rolled over the ship, and it began to fill with water.

The disciples became very frightened. They knew they were going to drown. But what was Jesus doing? He was sound asleep in the back of the ship.

"Lord, save us!" they shouted at Him. "We're about to die!" One of them said: "Master, don't You care if we drown?"

But Jesus looked up calmly at them and said: "Why are you so afraid? My, what a little faith you have!" A little more faith in Jesus and they wouldn't have been so afraid. They would have trusted in Him to take care of them.

Then Jesus got up and spoke to the wind and the waves. "Be quiet!" He said to the wind. "Be still," He said to the waves. At once the wind was quiet and the waves stopped rolling. Everything was very calm.

Storms on a lake can end very suddenly, but even then the waves keep on rolling for quite a while. When Jesus ordered the storm to stop, the wind stopped too, and the water became very still.

The men in the boat were afraid of Jesus when they saw what happened. They had seen Him heal sick people and drive devils out of others. But they didn't realize how powerful He really was. "What kind of a man is this?" they whispered. "Even the wind and the waves obey Him!"

Jesus rules everything in heaven and on earth. He isn't just another man. He is the almighty God. And He is Lord of the air and the ocean too.

Something more to think about: What sometimes makes us afraid in a bad storm? What can we do about this? Why were the disciples afraid when they saw how Jesus stopped the storm? How would we probably feel if we could suddenly see Jesus? Why? Why can we be sure that nothing will harm us as long as Jesus is with us?

Words to help us pray:

> As a mother stills her child,
> You can hush the ocean wild;
> Boisterous waves obey Your will
> When You say to them, "Be still!"
> Wondrous Ruler of the sea,
> Jesus, Savior, pilot me.

The Kind of Friends Jesus Chooses

The Bible says, "Jesus of Nazareth . . . went about doing good." In other words, when He was about 30 years old and had moved to Nazareth, He began traveling from one city to another. Wherever He went, He healed the sick and the crippled and the blind.

Jesus told the people that He was God's Son, who had

come to save them from their sins. He was bringing the kingdom of heaven to earth.

Many people followed Jesus wherever He went. Some who believed He was the Savior became Jesus' disciples. Others who thought they were good hated Jesus because He told them they were sinners. They didn't want a savior from their sins.

One day as Jesus was walking along, He saw a man called Matthew, a tax collector, sitting at work. Matthew collected the money people had to pay to their Roman rulers. Jesus walked up to Matthew and said, "Follow Me."

Matthew must have been very surprised when he heard Jesus say this, because in those days most Jews thought tax collectors were no good. They thought respectable people shouldn't even be friendly to Jews who collected taxes for the Romans. Matthew believed that Jesus was the promised Messiah. So he quit his job and went with Jesus. He was happy Jesus wanted him as a friend and partner in His work.

Later Matthew had a dinner for Jesus, His disciples, and many other people, some who had bad reputations. When the "goody-goodies" saw Jesus being friendly to Matthew and his friends, they said, "Why does Jesus eat with those sinners?"

Jesus heard them and answered, "People who are well don't need a doctor; only those who are sick need one. Go and learn what these words mean, 'I desire mercy and not sacrifices.' " Then He added, "I have come to help sinners, not people who think they are perfect."

Several days later Jesus called together His friends and chose 12 to be His special partners. One of the 12 was Matthew. After that Matthew left his home and went with Jesus wherever He went.

Something more to think about: Why did some people grumble when Jesus invited Matthew to join His group? All people are sinners. Jesus wants all people to enjoy God's forgiveness and love. Why, then, did He say He didn't want people who are perfect? What do you think God meant when He said in the Old Testament, "I desire mercy and not sacrifices"?

Words to help us pray: Dear Jesus, we're glad You chose some bad people to be Your friends and partners and that You said You came to save sinners. Make us kind and forgiving, as God is. Keep us from pretending we are good when we aren't. For Your name's sake we ask it. Amen.

Why Some Seeds Grow and Others Don't

One day Jesus told a story about a man who sowed some seeds and why some of them grew and others didn't:

A farmer went out to his field and sowed some seeds. He didn't have a tractor or a planting machine. He carried a bag of seeds over his shoulder and threw them on the ground as he walked along.

Some of the seeds fell on a hard path where they couldn't sink in and start to grow. Soon birds came along and ate them all up.

Some fell where there was only a little ground on top of hard rock. These seeds started to grow quickly, but the hard rock kept their little roots from growing. So when the weather got hot, the plants died. Their roots weren't very deep, and they couldn't find enough water.

Some of the farmer's seeds fell among weeds. The seeds grew, but the weeds grew faster. Then the weeds shut out the sunlight and took away the food and water the good plants needed. So they died too.

But some of the seeds fell on good ground. By and by the plants grew up and soon were producing grain. The size of the crop wasn't the same everywhere, but in the best places 100 times as much grain grew as was planted.

Later the disciples asked Jesus what this story meant. They knew He was trying to teach them something about God and life in God's kingdom. Jesus said, "The seed is the Word of God. It is planted whenever it is taught or preached. Those who hear the Word of God are like the ground on which the seed is sown.

"Some people are like the hard ground. They hear God's Word but don't understand it and don't even try to. So soon they forget what they hear. The Word of God can't even begin to grow in them.

"Some people who receive God's Word are like the rocky ground. For a little while they gladly believe it, but it doesn't sink in very deeply. So when they have troubles, they forget that God loves them.

"Those who hear and learn the Word of God but worry about making money and only think about having a good time are like the weedy ground. The worries and wants keep the Word of God from causing any good in their lives."

Finally Jesus talked about the seed that fell into good ground: "It's like people who hear God's message, think about it, and keep on believing it. In them God's word grows and produces many good results."

Something more to think about: According to this story, why does the teaching and learning of God's Word sometimes do us no good? What happens when the Word of God gets planted in different kinds of people? What are some of the good results that the message of God's love produces in us when we keep believing it?

Words to help us pray:
Almighty Father, bless the Word
Which through Your grace we now have heard.
Oh, may the precious seed take root,
Spring up, and bear abundant fruit!

A Girl Who Lived After She Died

In the country where Jesus lived, there was a man named Jairus, who had a young daughter. She was his only child, and he loved her very much.

One day she became very sick. Her mother and father knew she would soon die. Nothing seemed to help her. Then the father remembered what he had heard about Jesus and ran to find Him.

Jairus found Jesus talking to some of John's disciples. As usual, a big crowd was standing around. Jairus pushed through the crowd and knelt in front of Jesus. "My little daughter is very sick. Please come and lay Your hands on her so she will get well," he begged.

Well, Jesus went with Jairus right away. A lot of people followed them. But on the way a messenger came and told Jairus, "Your daughter has died. Don't bother the Teacher any longer."

When Jesus heard this, He said to Jairus, "Don't be afraid; believe, and your daughter will be well." And Jesus and Jairus went on.

When they came to Jairus' house, everyone was crying loudly because the girl was dead. "Don't cry," said Jesus. She isn't dead — she is only sleeping." Jesus meant that He could wake her up. Then all the people made fun of Jesus because they knew the girl was really dead.

But Jesus went into the girl's room and told everyone to leave except His three closest friends and the girl's parents. Then He took the girl's hand and said loudly, "Little girl, I say, get up!" As soon as Jesus said these words, she became alive again. And she opened her eyes and got up.

As you can imagine, her mother and father were so surprised, they didn't know what to do. Jesus even had to tell them to get their daughter something to eat. And then He told them not to tell anyone what He had done. But the news spread all over the country anyway.

Now you see that Jesus saves people not just from sin but also from death. He showed He could do that by making Jairus' little daughter alive again.

Another time Jesus said, "Whoever lives and believes in Me will never die." People who die while living with Jesus don't really die. They go on living with Jesus forever in heaven.

Something more to think about: Jesus told Jairus and his wife not to tell anyone He had made their dead daughter alive. Why? Why doesn't the Christian ever have to be afraid to die? What do we usually forget when someone we love dies? What will take away our tears?

Words to help us pray: Lord Jesus, thank You for showing us that You have the power to keep us alive. Help us remember, too, that when people who have Your love die, their life continues in heaven forever. For that we praise You. Amen.

The Time Jesus Fed a Big Crowd

Jesus had become famous. Big crowds were coming to hear Him preach about the kingdom of God. So many people brought their sick relatives to Jesus to be healed by Him that Jesus wanted some rest. "Let's go someplace where we'll be alone and can rest a while," He told His friends.

They got in a boat and started across a lake. But some of the people who saw them leave began following them on the shore. As they walked, many other people from the

45

towns along the way came out of their houses and went with them. Some took along sick persons, hoping Jesus would heal them.

When Jesus landed on the other side, He found a little hill where He could rest. But soon He saw the people coming and pitied them. So He spent the rest of the day healing the sick and talking about the heavenly Father's love.

Evening came, and Jesus' disciple Philip said to Him, "It's getting late. Send these people away so they can buy food for themselves in the villages."

But Jesus said to Philip, "You give them something to eat. Now where can we buy enough food to feed them all?" The Bible says that Jesus knew what He would do. But first He wanted to see how much Philip really trusted Him.

Philip answered, "Even for everyone to get just a little bit would take at least $200 worth of bread." Disciple Andrew said, "A boy here has five buns and two small fish. But that's not enough for so many people."

"Tell the people to sit down," Jesus said. So down they all sat on the grass, about 5,000 of them. Then Jesus took the boy's bread and fish and thanked His Father in heaven for the food. After that He passed it to His disciples and made it enough for everyone there.

Everybody ate as much as they wanted. Then Jesus said to His helpers, "Pick up what's left. Let's not waste anything." And they picked up 12 full baskets of food!

The people who saw what Jesus had done said, "This

certainly is the Savior who was to come to the world!" So they wanted to make Jesus their King right then and there. But Jesus didn't want to be that kind of king. And He went off into the hills.

Something more to think about: How does the power of God increase food for us? What didn't Philip realize? What should we know when we pray before eating, as Jesus did? Why didn't Jesus want the people to make Him their king right then and there? Jesus wanted to give the world something more important than free meals. Do you know what that is?

Words to help us sing:

> Praise God, from whom all blessings flow;
> Praise Him all creatures here below;
> Praise Him above, you heavenly host;
> Praise Father, Son, and Holy Ghost.

When Jesus Walked on Water

After Jesus fed a large crowd of people from a boy's lunch, some of them wanted to make Him their king. They thought He was powerful enough to drive the Romans out of their land. They also hoped He would rule over all Jews the way King Solomon had.

But Jesus wanted the people of His country and of the whole world to choose His kingdom in heaven. He wanted to be their Savior from sin. So when He saw that the people He had fed were about to make Him their king by force, He told His disciples to get into a ship and sail back across the lake. "I'll come later," He told them.

As the disciples did what Jesus told them to do, He hurried up into a mountain to get away from the people and to pray by Himself.

The boat sailed far out on the lake, and it was dark. Suddenly a strong wind started blowing. Then the waves began to roll. Soon the boat tossed up and down, and the disciples forgot how Jesus had stopped the storm once before. All night long they tried hard to row to shore, but the big waves were against them.

When they were about to give up and thought they would drown, they saw something moving over the water. Jesus was coming to help them. He was walking right on top of the water. That really scared them.

"It's a ghost!" they hollered.

"It's all right. Don't be afraid. It's Jesus," Jesus called to them.

When Peter heard Jesus, he got a little braver and wanted to go to Him. "Lord, if it's really You," he said, "order me to walk to You on the water." "Come," said Jesus. So Peter climbed out of the ship and actually walked on the water!

But when he saw a large wave rushing at him, he lost his nerve and started to sink. "Save me, Lord!" he screamed. Jesus reached out, grabbed Peter, and pulled him up. Then He said to Peter, "My, what a little faith you have. Why didn't you believe what I said? I told you, you could walk on the water."

After Peter and Jesus walked to the ship and climbed in, Jesus again made the wind die down. The disciples were amazed at Jesus' power. They knelt down in front of Him and said, "You are truly the Son of God."

Something more to think about: What do you think Jesus prayed about when He left the people He had fed? Why didn't He let the people make Him their king? Why is it that people often think they see ghosts when they are very scared? What did the disciples forget even though

they had seen Jesus' power that day? Why did Peter start
to sink? How did Jesus save him?

Words to help us pray:

      Jesus, Savior, come to me;
      Let me ever be with Thee.
      Come and nevermore depart,
      Thou who reignest in my heart.
               Amen.

The Story of a Very Good Shepherd

A shepherd is a man who takes care of sheep. In the morning he leads his flock to pastures of green grass. When a hungry wolf comes along, he calls his sheep together. Then he risks his own life to defend them.

In the evening shepherds bring their sheep into a fold, a place with a wall around it. The different sheep mix together. But in the morning each shepherd calls his sheep, and they follow their own shepherd.

Jesus once said, "I am the Good Shepherd, and I know My sheep, and they know Me." What did He mean? He meant that He knows everyone who loves Him and belongs to Him.

And believers know Jesus, their Shepherd, too. They follow Him. When they do, He takes care of them and protects them from the devil, who is like a wolf.

Jesus also told a story about a lost sheep to show how much He and His Father in heaven love us: "What do you think a good shepherd who has 100 sheep will do when one of them gets lost?" He asked.

"He will leave the 99 sheep in the pasture and will go looking for the lost one. He'll look and look until he finds it. Then, when he finds the lost sheep, he is very happy. He puts it on his shoulders and carries it back home. He calls his neighbors together and says, 'I have found my lost sheep! Let's celebrate.' "

Long before Jesus came and said, "I am the Good Shepherd," King David wrote a psalm that says, "The Lord is my Shepherd." Because God is our Good Shepherd, we can say the rest of David's psalm:

"I shall not want. He makes me lie down in green pastures. He leads me beside the still waters. . . . Surely goodness and mercy will follow me all the days of my life, and I will live in the house of the Lord forever."

Something more to think about: What was Jesus saying about Himself and God when He told the story about the Good Shepherd? How can Jesus' sheep hear and recognize His voice? What do His lambs and sheep do when they really belong to Him? Jesus said, "A good shepherd gives his life for his sheep." How did Jesus do that?

Words that help us sing:

> Seeing I am Jesus' lamb,
> Ever glad at heart I am;
> For my Shepherd gently guides me,
> Knows my need and well provides me,
> Loves me every day the same,
> Even calls me by my name.

How Great Jesus Is!

One day Jesus asked His disciples, "Who do people say the Son of Man is?" Calling Himself "the Son of Man" was a little like saying to people, "I'm one of you, and I'm for you." Some Christians call Him a "true man" because He really was a human being.

The disciples answered Jesus, "Some say You are John the Baptizer. Others say You are Elijah. Still others say Jeremiah or some other prophet."

"And what about you? Who do you say I am?" Jesus asked.

Simon Peter answered, "You are the Messiah, the Son of the living God."

"Good for you, Simon," said Jesus. "You didn't learn that from people but from My Father, who is in heaven. You are a rock, Peter. On this rock I will build My church."

From that day on Jesus talked to His disciples about going to Jerusalem and about being put to death and rising again on the third day. This bothered Peter. So he took Jesus by the arm and said to Him, "This must never happen to You!"

"Get away from Me, devil! What you're telling me isn't what God wants," Jesus shouted at Peter.

Six days later Jesus took Peter, his brother James, and

John with Him to the top of a high mountain. There Jesus began to pray. But the disciples started getting very sleepy.

Suddenly they saw Him start to change. His face and clothes began to shine as bright as the sun. And then two dead men, Moses and Elijah, appeared and started talking with Him. By this time the three sleepy disciples were wide awake.

"How wonderful!" Peter thought. "It's like looking into heaven." So Peter said to Jesus, "Lord, it's good to be here. Let me make three houses, one for You, one for Moses, and one for Elijah." Peter wanted to stay there on the mountain.

But while Peter was talking, a bright cloud came over Jesus and His friends. Then a voice said from the cloud: "This is My Son. I love Him and am pleased with Him. Listen to Him!" At that the disciples fell to the ground and lay there shaking.

Then Jesus came out of the cloud, put His hand on His friends, and said, "Get up. Don't be afraid." When they looked up they saw only Jesus.

Well, Peter, James, and John never forgot what they saw there on the mountain. Jesus was much more than just a great, good man. He was God's Son, the King of heaven. And now He had come from heaven to be the promised Savior of the world.

Something more to think about: Why did Jesus call Simon Peter a rock? Why did Jesus call Peter a devil right after that? How did what happened on the mountain make Peter's faith stronger? Why were the disciples afraid of what they heard? Why don't we ever have to be afraid of God if we are friends of Jesus?

Words to help us pray: God, we have seen Your glory in Your Son Jesus. Make His love shine in our faces and lives. Then through us others will see how wonderful He is. Amen.

What Happens When We Don't Forgive

Peter once asked Jesus, "How often must I forgive a person who harms me? Is seven times enough?"

"No, not just seven times, but 70 times seven," Jesus answered. Then He told a story:

A king asked all his servants to pay what they owed him. But one servant owed him so much that he could never pay it all back. So the king said, "Sell this man, his family, and everything he owns. Then I'll get back at least some of what he owes me."

When the servant heard this, he flopped down on his knees in front of the king. "Please give me more time; then I will pay you everything I owe you," he begged. The king felt sorry for his servant, who could never pay back the debt. So he forgave the man everything he owed and set him free.

Well, you'd think that servant would have been happy and would have told everyone how kind and good the king

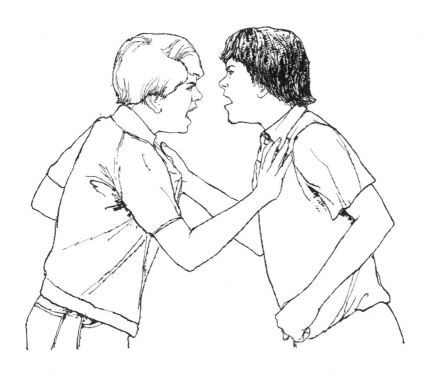

had been to him. But on the way home he met a friend who owed him just a few dollars. He grabbed his friend by the throat and yelled, "You pay me what you owe me!"

"Please give me a little time," the friend begged, "and I'll pay you." But the unforgiving servant wouldn't wait. Instead, he had his friend thrown into jail.

When the kind king heard what the unforgiving servant had done, he became very angry. He called that servant and said to him, "You wicked fellow! I forgave you everything just because you asked me to. Now why didn't you forgive your friend?" Then the king put the unforgiving servant in jail until he would pay back all he owed.

After telling this story, Jesus said, "That is how my Father in heaven will treat you if you do not forgive."

Something more to think about: How many times did Jesus mean by saying 70 times seven? Why does Jesus, our God and King, expect us to forgive as many times as a person asks us to forgive him? What does our not forgiving some other person say we believe about forgiveness? Why is there no limit to God's forgiveness?

Words to help us pray: Dear Father in heaven, our Lord and King, forgive us our sins and make us willing to forgive those who sin against us. As followers of Jesus we ask it. Amen.

How to Love a Neighbor

Once a lawyer came to Jesus and asked, "What must I do to get eternal life?" Jesus answered, "What do the Scriptures say?"

The man said, "You must love the Lord your God with all your heart and with all your soul and with all your mind, and you must love your neighbor as yourself." Jesus said to the lawyer, "You're right. Do this and you will live."

But the lawyer asked, "Who is my neighbor?" So Jesus told him this story:

While a man was on a trip, some robbers jumped on him. They beat him up, took his money and clothes, and left him just about dead.

After a while a priest came walking along the road. He saw the man who was hurt, but walked right on by. Soon another man walked up and took a look at the victim, but then hurried away.

Finally a man from Samaria came by with his donkey. In those days the Jews weren't very nice to Samaritans, but when this Samaritan saw the hurt Jew, he felt sorry for him. He put some oil on the man's cuts and bandaged his wounds. Then he put the Jew on the donkey and took him to an inn, a place something like a motel.

All that night he took care of the Jew. The next morning the Samaritan had to leave. But he gave the man who ran the inn some money. "Take care of the hurt Jew," he said. "If you need more money, I'll pay you on my way back."

After Jesus finished telling this story, He asked the lawyer, "Which of the three men acted like a good neighbor to the man hurt by the robbers?" The lawyer answered, "The one who was kind." Jesus said, "Then go and be kind too."

Several other times Jesus said to His disciples, "You have heard it said, 'Love your friends; hate your enemies.' But I am telling you to love your enemies, do good to those who hate you, and pray for those who are bad to you. Why should you receive a blessing for loving only the people who love you? Even wicked people love those who love them! And even sinners do good to those who do good to them. Why should you be blessed for that?"

Something more to think about: The Bible says that the lawyer was trying to trap Jesus. Since the lawyer knew God's laws, why did he ask what he must do to have life with God forever? What did he probably think he was already doing? What did the story teach the lawyer about God and His kind of life? How can we get the power to love even those who don't love us?

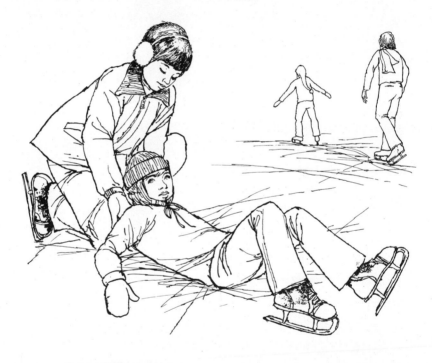

Words to help us pray: Lord Jesus, our Good Samaritan, we can never thank You enough for having pity on us and for giving us Your life. Help us to help anybody in need and to love them as we love ourselves. Then we will truly be Your followers. Amen.

What Pleases Jesus the Most

Two of Jesus' closest friends were sisters named Mary and Martha. They lived together in a little town called Bethany, where Jesus often stopped on His way to or from Jerusalem.

One time, as soon as Jesus and His disciples stopped at Mary and Martha's home, Martha started fixing a meal for them. She thought the best thing she could do was get some food on the table as fast as possible.

But Mary thought it was more important to sit by Jesus and visit with Him. She enjoyed hearing Jesus talk about God and what God wanted Jesus and His friends to do for the world.

While they talked, Martha was having trouble. She got pretty upset because she couldn't get dinner ready fast enough all by herself. There was all that food to prepare, and Mary was just sitting and listening to Jesus!

When Martha couldn't stand it any longer, she came to Jesus and said, "Lord, don't You care that my sister has left all the work for me? Tell her to come and help! I need her in the kitchen."

When Jesus heard this, He felt sorry for Martha. He

knew she meant well and was trying to make His visit pleasant. But Martha didn't understand what was most important — more important even than food.

Looking at Martha, Jesus said sort of sadly, "Martha, oh, Martha, you get upset over so many things. But only one thing is really needed." All she really had to do to enjoy Jesus' company was to sit down and visit with Him.

Then Jesus added, "Mary chose the best thing. Don't take it away from her." So Jesus wasn't willing to make Mary work in the kitchen as long as she wanted to sit and listen to Him.

Something more to think about: Both Mary and Martha loved Jesus, but what lesson did Martha have to learn? What did Jesus mean when He said, "Only one thing is really needed"? How did Jesus often show that nothing was ever more important than the Word of God?

Words to help us pray: Dear Jesus, our Lord and Savior, help us always give first place to You and Your Word of God's love. Then we will be most blessed. We ask this for Your name's sake. Amen.

A Story of a Fig Tree

As you perhaps know, figs are a kind of fruit. They grow on trees and grow especially well in the country where Jesus lived.

One day Jesus told a story about a fig tree: A man had a fig tree growing in his yard. When it was time for the tree to have figs, he came looking for them, but found none. All the tree had on its branches was leaves.

A fruit tree, to be any good, is supposed to grow fruit. So the man went and talked to his gardener about the fig tree: "For 3 years I've been looking for figs on this tree and I've never found any. Now cut it down! Why waste the ground for such a worthless tree?"

But the gardener didn't want to cut it down. He said, "Sir, please leave the tree just 1 more year. I'll put fer-

tilizer around it and take special care of it. Then if figs grow on the tree, good. But if they don't, I'll cut it down.''

Well, Jesus didn't finish that story. He didn't tell us if the fig tree was saved. Maybe He wanted us to finish the story for ourselves.

In order to do that, we have to know what Jesus was talking about. The fig tree stands for people—anyone in God's garden. The lord or owner is God. The gardener is Jesus. He wants to save all the trees in God's garden.

God the Father, the owner, wants to see His trees produce fruit. He doesn't want trees that just look good.

Jesus, the gardener, is willing to dig up the hard ground

around the trees and put fertilizer on them so they will bear good fruit. The Word of God is the fertilizer. It makes the trees more alive.

Now, if you had been the fig tree in the story, would you have been saved?

Something more to think about: The Bible often talks about the fruits of faith. Fruits of faith are what faith in Jesus produces in a person's life. What do you think some of these fruits are? If a person says he believes in Jesus but does not do what God wants him to do, he is like a fruit tree without fruit. Why is God not pleased with such people? How long is Jesus willing to try to save us?

Words to help us pray: Dear Jesus, make us produce a lot of good fruit for You. Water and fertilize us with Your teachings and Your Spirit. For Your name's sake we ask it. Amen.

A Supper to Which We're All Invited

In talking to people about God and the kingdom of heaven, Jesus often made up stories. These stories are called parables because they teach by com-*par*-ing something not known to something well known.

One day Jesus told a story about a king who prepared a big supper to celebrate his son's wedding. The king invited many people to the feast.

When the feast was ready, the king sent his servants to tell the guests that it was time to come. But they didn't want to come.

They all made excuses. One said, "I bought a field and have to go and look it over. Please excuse me." Another one said, "I bought five pairs of oxen and am on my way to try them out. Please excuse me." And another said, "I just got married. I can't come."

Well, the servants went back and told all this to the king, who was furious. He said, "My wedding feast is ready, but the people I invited didn't deserve it. So go out to the streets and alleys of the town and invite everyone you see."

The servants went out and invited all the people they could find, good and bad alike. When the king heard there was still room, he said to his servants, "Go out to the country and get anybody you can find to come. My house will be full. But nobody who refused to come will get even a taste of my supper." And before the evening was over, the king's house was filled.

Later the king came to take a look at the guests and saw a man who didn't have on wedding clothes. Because in those days a king gave his guests robes to wear, he said to that man, "Friend, how did you get in here without wearing your wedding clothes?" And the man said nothing, because he knew he should have put them on. Then the king said to his servants, "Throw this fellow out into the dark night."

This parable is about heaven. Can you guess how it

is like what happens in heaven? The king is God, our Father in heaven. And you know who His Son is. What are some of the good things God has prepared for all who come to His Son's wedding?

Something more to think about: Why do some people still refuse God's invitation to enjoy His banquet of love and peace? What excuses do we make nowadays for not coming to God's house to celebrate His Son's wedding? Like the king, God gives a wedding robe to all His guests so that their dirty clothes are covered up and they can look presentable. Do you know how God does that?

Words to help us pray: Heavenly Father, our God and King, we thank You for having invited everyone, including us, to the great supper of blessings You have prepared. Make us glad to celebrate the wedding of Your Son, Jesus, to His church. Cover our sins with the wedding clothes of His forgiveness and love. For His sake we ask it. Amen.

How Good God Really Is

Jesus wanted people to know what God is like, so one day He told this story:

There was a man who had two sons. The sons had a good father and a good life at home, but the younger son wanted to leave. So he said to his father, "Father, give me my share of your property, and let me go and live by myself."

Well, the father loved his son and didn't want him to leave. But he also didn't want to make his son stay with him. So he divided all his property and gave the younger son his part.

After a few days the younger son sold his property and left home. He took all his money with him and spent part of it getting to a faraway country. There he wasted the rest of it on foolish living.

When his money was all gone, he couldn't buy any food. Because there was a big food shortage at that time, a famine, no one would give a stranger anything to eat. Finally the young son went to work taking care of pigs for a farmer.

He got so hungry that he wished he could eat the pig food. Then one day as he was watching the pigs, he began to think of what a nice home he had left and of his good, kind father. He said to himself, "All my father's servants have more than they can eat, and here I am starving."

"I will go back to my father," he decided, "and will say to him, 'Father, I have sinned against God and against you. I don't deserve to be called your son. But please make me one of your servants.'" Then he got up and started home.

He was still quite a ways from the house when his father, who often looked up and down the road for him, saw him coming. As soon as he saw his son, he ran to him, threw his arms around him, and kissed him.

"Father," the son said, "I have sinned against God and against you. I don't deserve to be called your son anymore." But the father was happy just to have his son back. He shouted to his servants, "Hurry and bring the best robe we have and put it on him, and put a ring on his finger and shoes on his feet. Then let us eat and be merry. This son of mine was dead, but now he is alive again."

Something more to think about: What do you think Jesus is trying to teach us about God? Why did the father gladly forgive and forget what his son had done? How do you think the son must have felt when his father welcomed him back the way he did?

Words to help us sing:

> Amazing grace! How sweet the sound
> That saved a fool like me!
> I once was lost, but now am found,
> Was blind, but now I see!

How Much Life with God Is Worth

When God rules people, He is their Lord and King and they are citizens in His kingdom. God's kingdom is not any one country. It is wherever there are people in whom God's Spirit lives.

Jesus gave us many pictures of what the kingdom of God and life in it are like. He told longer stories, like the parable of the king who forgave his servant everything he owed, or the father who welcomed back his son. And He gave very short examples from nature: "God's kingdom is like a tiny mustard seed. Out of a mustard seed grows a big tree with many branches," He said.

Jesus also told stories to show the importance and value of life with God. One very short but very important story is about a man who found a buried treasure in a field. See if you can guess what it teaches.

The kingdom of heaven is like a treasure buried in a field. A man discovered it while plowing the ground. It probably was money and sparkling jewels in an old treasure chest. Whatever it was, the man jumped for joy because he knew how valuable his new treasure was.

The man was very wise. He quickly covered the chest and went and sold everything he had. Then he went to the person who owned the field and offered to buy it from him. You see, he knew what a great treasure was buried there and what it was worth. So he was willing to give up all he owned to get hold of that treasure.

Jesus also said that the kingdom of heaven is like a buyer of fine pearls who looked and looked for the most beautiful pearl of all. When he finally found it, he went and sold everything he owned so he could buy the one perfect pearl.

Perfect pearls are still worth a lot. They are found inside oyster shells and are used for rings and beads. But can you imagine a pearl so lovely that you'd give up all your things just to have it?

Jesus wasn't talking about a pearl for a ring or a necklace. The pearl He was talking about is life with God. How much do you think life with God is worth? What could be worth more than life with God?

Something more to think about: What are some of the things people value most? How do we show what we value? What was Jesus trying to tell us when He told about the treasure in the field and the costly pearl? Why is life with God worth more than anything else we own? What are we willing to give up in order to have this life?

Words to help us pray: Dear Father in heaven, we're glad we found the life Jesus gives. Make us willing to give up anything that will keep You from ruling in our hearts and lives, through Jesus, our Savior. Amen.

The People Who Are Tops with Jesus

Some people worry a lot about who is most important in a group and whether they will become important and powerful.

One day on a trip Jesus' disciples were arguing about who would be the most important in Jesus' heavenly kingdom. Some of them probably thought they would be His favorites and would get to rule other people.

Back home that night Jesus asked them, "What were you arguing about on the road?" They were ashamed of themselves and didn't answer at first. But then they asked, "Who is the greatest in the kingdom of heaven?"

Jesus must have shaken His head sadly. He sat down and said, "Whoever wants to be first must put himself last and must be the servant of all the others." Jesus had often said, "If anyone wants to be really great, he must be the servant of the rest."

Then Jesus called a child over to stand by Him. "Remember this!" said Jesus. "Unless you change and become like children, you will never even get into the kingdom of heaven. The greatest person in the kingdom of heaven is the one who becomes humble like this child!"

Do you have any idea what Jesus meant by being humble? The little child didn't feel great or important. He was just happy being alive and having Jesus as a friend.

Then Jesus did something else to show what children are like and how much He loves them. He held the child close and said, "Whoever loves and cares for such a child for My sake will be loving Me; and whoever loves and serves Me also loves and serves the One who sent Me."

A little later Jesus said, "Be careful that you don't ever think one of these little ones is unimportant. They have angels who are always near My Father in heaven." That's the way Jesus tried to show how important children are to God.

Something more to think about: Why do most of us often worry about who is the greatest? From what you've read, what kind of people does Jesus consider the greatest? How was the little child a great Christian? What did Jesus say to show how important children are to God?

Words to help us pray: Dear Jesus, forgive us for making ourselves great at the expense of others. Help us understand that in God's eyes the greatest people are those who gladly serve others. Make us all like children who are happy to have Your love and enjoy giving Your love to others. Amen.

How Jesus Feels About Children

We heard what Jesus said about children, especially those who believe in Him. A little later He also showed that He meant what He said. It happened while Jesus was on His way to the part of His country called Judea.

When Jesus stopped in a village to rest a bit, some mothers heard that this great Man of God was in their town. They thought, "Oh, if we could get to touch Him and get Him to touch our children! What a blessing that would be!" You know how proud some people get when a famous man puts his hand on their child.

So the mothers took their children to see Jesus. They even brought their babies. But when the disciples saw them coming to bother Jesus, they became angry. They scolded the mothers for trying to present their children to Jesus and told them to go away.

When Jesus saw what the disciples were doing, He became angry. "Let the children come to Me and don't

tell them they can't. To such belong the kingdom of God,"
He said. The life and kingdom He was bringing was especially right for children.

And then Jesus said what He had said once before:
"Remember this! Whoever does not accept the kingdom
of God like a little child does will never enter it." It takes
the faith of a child to enjoy the love and life of God in His
kingdom of heaven. Then Jesus took the little children in
His arms, touched each of them, talked to them, and
blessed them.

Jesus is pleased when parents bring their children to
Him for His blessing. He *wants* them to do so and wants
children in His kingdom.

Parents bring their children to Jesus when they teach

them about Jesus and His love. They also bring their children to Jesus in church. Jesus said, "Where two or three of my friends and followers get together in My name, there I am also."

Something more to think about: How do we know that all children are very important to Jesus? Jesus no longer is visible and in any one place; now He is everywhere. How can children go to Him these days to be blessed by Him? Why did Jesus say that older people had to become like children in order to be in His kingdom?

Words to help us pray: Dear Jesus, we're happy You showed us how You love children. Keep us all close to You so that we may live with You in heaven, both now and forever. In Your name we ask this. Amen.

A Lesson on How and Why to Pray

"Suppose a friend who is on a trip comes to your house at midnight, but you don't have any food to serve him. So you go to another friend living nearby, and you knock and say to him, 'Please lend me three loaves of bread. Another friend of mine has just arrived in town, and I don't have anything to feed him.'

"What if that friend answers from inside his house, 'Don't bother me! I've locked the door already, and we're all in bed.' What then?"

Jesus asked and answered that question once after He had been praying. "Even if the friend won't give you the bread just to be friendly, he will get up and give you what you need just to get you to be quiet," said Jesus.

"Ask and you will receive; seek and you will find; knock and the door will be opened to you. For everyone who asks, receives; whoever searches, finds; and doors are opened for the person who knocks."

A little later Jesus told a parable about a judge. This story shows how we should keep on praying:

"There was once a judge who cared nothing about God or other people. He wasn't a bit interested in listening to people's troubles. And he never went out of his way to help anyone.

"In the judge's town lived a widow who kept coming to him. Someone was trying to take away her property and her rights. Again and again she went to the judge saying, "Won't you please help me against my enemy."

For a while the judge refused to do anything for the woman. Then, finally, he said to himself, "I don't care anything about God or other people. Still, I'd better see to it that this woman gets her rights. Otherwise she will keep bothering me and just wear me out."

When Jesus finished telling this story, He explained the lesson He was trying to teach. "Remember what the no-good judge said and did. He helped the widow because she kept pestering him. Now, if someone like that judge will help a person who pesters him, don't you think God will help His children who cry to Him for help day and night? Believe Me," said Jesus, "God will help them very quickly."

Something more to think about: The widow in the story is like all of us. Our main enemy is the devil. What rights and blessings does the devil try to take from us? Why wasn't the judge in the story willing to help the widow? Why is God always willing to Help His children? Why, then, should we keep on praying, even when God doesn't answer our prayer right away?

Words to help us pray: We thank You, Father in heaven and Judge of all things, that through faith in Jesus we are Your children. We know You will answer our prayers. Keep us praying for all You have promised us. Through Jesus Christ, our Lord. Amen.

Three Kinds of Servants

Jesus once told the following story. It teaches us how to use the gifts He gives us.

A rich man was about to go on a trip. Before leaving he had a meeting with his servants and put them in charge of his property and business. He also gave each one some money to work with while he was gone.

He gave one of the servants $5,000, another $2,000, and a third, $1,000. Then he went away on his trip.

The servant with the $5,000 went at once and put his

money to work. We don't know exactly what he did with it. Perhaps he bought another home and rented it, or maybe he bought another business for his lord. Soon he earned $5,000 more. And the servant with the $2,000 earned another $2,000.

But the servant who had received only $1,000 didn't earn any more with it. Instead he buried his master's money in the ground.

When the master came back, he called the three servants to him and said, "What did you do with the money I let you use while I was gone?"

The servant who had received $5,000 stepped forward and said, "Here is the $5,000 you gave me, and here is *another* $5,000 that I earned with it." To that the master said, "Well done, good and faithful servant. You did a good job managing small amounts. Now I will put you in charge of large amounts. Come and be my happy partner."

Next, the servant who had been given $2,000 came forward and said, "You gave me $2,000. Here it is. And here is another $2,000 that I earned with your money." Again the master said, "Well done, good and faithful servant. You did just fine managing small amounts; now I will put you in charge of large amounts. Come and be my happy partner."

Then the master asked the servant who had received $1,000, "And what have you done with my gift to you?"

"Sir, I know you are a hard man," he began. "You even expect crops where you haven't planted seeds. So I was afraid. I hid your money in the ground. See! Here is what belongs to you. I kept it safe while you were gone."

"You good-for-nothing servant!" the master said. "At least you should have put my money in a bank. Then I would have gotten a little interest. Because you didn't use what I gave you, I will take your $1,000 and give it to the servant who has $10,000."

Something more to think about: Our master is Jesus Christ. He has gone away for a while. But before He left, He put us in charge of His business and work. He gives all His servants some gifts to work with. What are some He has given you? How can you use them for His benefit? What do you think Jesus was trying to teach by telling this story?

Words to help us pray: Lord Jesus, thank You for giving us the Gospel of God's love and forgiveness. Don't ever let us bury it and try to keep it safe for ourselves. Make us good managers of all Your gifts, so that Your business and kingdom will grow. Amen.

Why Jesus Stayed with a Man Named Zacchaeus

One day Jesus and His disciples were passing through a city called Jericho, where a man named Zacchaeus lived. He was the chief tax collector for the Romans who ruled that country.

Most tax collectors, also called publicans, were thieves. They cheated the people and the government. Zacchaeus, too, had been a rotten politician and had gotten very rich.

But Zacchaeus was sad and lonely because he knew he had done wrong. His own people hated him and left him all alone.

When the people of Jericho heard that Jesus was in town, they hurried to see Him. They knew about Jesus' claim to be the promised Savior of God's people and about His miracles.

Zacchaeus, too, wanted to see Jesus. But he was a short little man and couldn't see over the crowd. "I just must see this Jesus," said Zacchaeus to himself. So he ran ahead of the people who were walking with Jesus and climbed into a tree. There he sat waiting for Jesus to pass by.

Jesus walked under Zacchaeus' tree, looked up, and said to the little man, "Zacchaeus, climb down quickly. I must stay in your house today." Well, it didn't take Zacchaeus long to get down from that tree. Happily he invited Jesus to stay at his home. Then he took Him there.

But you can guess what else happened. All the people who saw Jesus go home with Zacchaeus started grumbling. "This man has gone to the home of a sinner!" they said. But Jesus had done this on purpose: He is the Friend and Savior of very bad people too.

Later at his house Zacchaeus did what everyone does who finds the love and forgiveness of God. He told

Jesus he was sorry for all the things he had done wrong. Then he promised Jesus, "I've decided to give half of all I own to the poor. And if I've cheated anyone, I'll give him back four times as much as I took."

When Jesus saw how eager Zacchaeus was to do what was right and good, He said, "Today salvation has come to this house. For I came to look for and save the lost."

Something more to think about: Can you think of persons so bad that Jesus doesn't love them? Why were many of the people upset when they saw that Jesus went home with Zacchaeus? Why was Zacchaeus willing to change into an unselfish and really good person? Is Jesus living with you?

Words to help us pray:

You have promised to receive us,
Poor and sinful though we be;
You give mercy to relieve us
And the power to be free.
Blessed Jesus,
Give Your grace and power to me. Amen.

God's Way of Doing Things

Jesus once told a story to show that God gives people more than they deserve. That is what God's grace is — undeserved love and blessings.

Once a landlord went to a village early in the morning to hire some men to work for him. He promised to pay them what they usually got, a silver coin for a day's work. When they agreed to the salary, he sent them off to work in his vineyard.

Later, at 9 o'clock, the landlord went back to the village and saw some other men standing around doing nothing. "Go work in my vineyard," he said, "and whatever is right I will pay you." So they went to work, planting grapevines or maybe picking grapes.

Then at 12 o'clock and again at 3 in the afternoon the

landlord did the same thing. At about 5 he went to the village and saw a few others still standing around doing nothing. "Why in the world have you been standing here all day doing nothing?" he asked. "Because no one hired us," they answered. "Well, then," said the landlord, "go and work in my vineyard as long as you can."

When evening came, the owner of the vineyard said to his foreman, "Call the workers and pay them their wages. Begin with those we hired last and end with those who were hired first." When those who had been hired about 5 o'clock came, they each received a full day's pay—a silver coin! So did all the other part-time workers.

Then the men who were the first to be hired came.

They thought they would receive more. But they too were given a silver coin for their work. And that started them grumbling. "These men who were hired last worked only 1 hour, and we put up with a whole day's work in this hot sun. Still you paid them the same as you paid us!" they complained.

To that the owner replied, "Friends, I am doing you no wrong. You agreed to work a day for a silver coin, didn't you? So take your pay and go. Don't I have the right to do what I want with what I own? Or don't you want me to be generous? I wanted to give the last man hired as much as I gave you."

After that Jesus said something He had told Peter once before: "Those who are last will be first, and the first will be last." Our God doesn't pay people according to what they have done or what they deserve. He treats people out of the goodness of His heart.

Something more to think about: When Jesus talked about the people who were hired at the beginning of the day, He probably meant the Jews in Old Testament times. They had served God a long time. Why didn't that make them more deserving than people who entered God's kingdom later? Why are we least likely to get God's gifts when we think we are first and deserve the most?

Words to help us pray: Lord God, we thank You for inviting us to work in Your kingdom. Give us Your Holy Spirit, Lord, so that we won't serve You for pay, but cheerfully because of Your grace in Jesus Christ, our Savior. Amen.

What Kind of Giving Do You Do?

Some children think that because they don't have much to give they don't have to give anything to God or to people who need help. But the person who always gets and seldom gives isn't as happy as he would be in giving. That's why Jesus said, "It's more blessed to give than to receive." And it isn't the size or the amount of the gift that matters to God.

Jesus and His disciples had gone to the temple in Jerusalem, as they often did. There Jesus sat down in one of the courtyards and watched people putting money in the collection boxes. The money was used to take care of God's house and God's servants, the priests.

Rich people who came put quite a bit of money into the boxes. Many others gave just a little. And except for those who gave just to show off, what Jesus saw pleased Him.

But there was one gift that pleased Jesus more than

any other. As He sat there watching, a poor widow came by. She didn't have a husband to earn money and take care of her. Still, she quietly dropped two copper coins into one of the boxes. They were worth about a penny.

When Jesus saw what the poor woman had given, He called His disciples together and said to them, "See that poor widow over there? She put more into the offering box than any of the others."

"But she only gave two copper coins," said one of the men. "The others gave pieces of gold and silver." To that Jesus replied, "Yes, but the others put in only a small part of their riches — what they could easily spare. This poor widow put in all she had and even what she needed for herself."

Jesus is interested in what we give. And it's never the amount we give that decides the value. It's a question of how much we give of what we have. And of course the reasons we give and how we feel when we give also matter to God. The Bible says, "God loves a cheerful giver."

Something more to think about: Why do some people never want to give anything to anybody, even to their church? Why is a giver happier than a receiver? Why was Jesus more pleased with the woman's small gift than with the large ones He saw people giving? Why wouldn't a small gift of a penny please God if we could give more?

Words to help us pray: Dear Father in heaven, You give us much that we can give back to You. Make us happy to share Your love by giving to Your church and to the needy. For the sake of Jesus we ask this. Amen.

The People Who Never Really Die

You probably remember the sisters Mary and Martha. Jesus enjoyed stopping at their house whenever He came to the town of Bethany. They were His good friends.

Mary and Martha had a brother named Lazarus, who also lived in Bethany. One day Lazarus became very sick. When it looked like he might die, the sisters sent a message to Jesus: "Lord, the friend You love is sick."

When Jesus got the message He said, "This has happened so that God and His Son will receive glory." But then, instead of going to Bethany right away, Jesus deliberately stayed where He was for 2 more days.

At the end of the 2 days Jesus said to His disciples, "Our friend Lazarus has fallen asleep, but I will go and wake him up." One of the disciples said, "If he is asleep, Lord, he will get well." But Jesus meant that Lazarus had died. So He explained, "Lazarus is dead, but we'll go to him."

Just outside the town of Bethany a man told Jesus, "Lazarus died 4 days ago." When Martha heard Jesus was coming, she hurried out to meet Him. "If You had been here, my brother wouldn't have died," she said.

"Your brother will rise again," Jesus said to Martha.

"I know he will rise to life again on the last day of the world," said Martha. Then Jesus explained to her, "I am the Resurrection and the Life. Whoever believes in Me will never die. Martha, do you believe this?"

"Yes, Lord. I believe You are the Savior, the Son of God, who has come into the world," she said.

Then Martha ran back to tell Mary that Jesus was coming. And Mary ran out to meet Him. Many people in the house with Mary ran after her. They thought she was going back to her brother's grave. There was quite a commotion.

When Jesus saw Mary and all her friends crying, He cried too. "Where have you buried Lazarus?" Jesus asked. They took Him to a cave shut up by a big stone. "Take the stone away," said Jesus.

Then Jesus looked up and said, "Father, I thank You

that You listen to Me. Now the people here will believe that You sent Me." Then He shouted, "Lazarus, come out!"

As the weepy people stood staring at the grave, Lazarus walked out, all wrapped up like a mummy. You can imagine what the people thought! But Jesus said, "Unwrap him so he can go home." Oh, how thankful Mary and Martha were. They knew whoever believes in Jesus never really dies.

Something more to think about: Jesus showed He had the power to call dead people back to life. He also said that all who believe in Him never really die. They go on living with Him in heaven. Why is this a wonderful and great thing to know?

Words to help us pray: Dear Jesus, we're glad You have the power to bring people out of death to life. Give us eternal life with You in heaven. In Your name we ask it. Amen.

A Sick Child Jesus Healed

One day Jesus went back to the little town of Cana in the country where He grew up. Once He had changed some water into wine there. The people welcomed Him because many had seen and heard Him in the temple in Jerusalem. He was becoming famous for what He taught and did.

In another town called Capernaum, in that same country, lived a government official whose son was very sick. The man loved his boy and was afraid he might die. Like most parents, he was willing to do almost anything to get help for his child.

When this man heard that Jesus was in Cana, he decided to go and ask Him to come and make his boy well. He believed that Jesus had the power of God to heal sicknesses.

When the man came and asked, Jesus said to him, "You all have to see miracles before you believe." Jesus was testing the man's faith.

"Sir, please come with me before my child dies," the official begged. He didn't want to see a miracle; he wanted the son he loved to get well.

So Jesus said to him, "Go back to your home. Your son will live." That was another test of the man's faith in Jesus. Would he believe what Jesus said? The Bible says he did and he went home. He knew Jesus didn't have to be there to heal his son.

On his way home the man met some of his servants. They were coming to find him and were all excited to tell him the good news. "Your boy is going to live!" they said as soon as they saw him. "He's much, much better."

The report was almost too good to believe. "When did he begin to get well?" the man asked his servants excitedly. "Yesterday at 1 o'clock his fever went down," they answered.

Then the father remembered that this was exactly

the time when Jesus told him, "Your son will live." You can bet he hurried home. He wanted to see his boy. And he wanted to tell his family about Jesus, the One who made the boy well.

That man and all his family believed in Jesus. They didn't only believe that Jesus healed the boy. They also believed that Jesus was God's Son, the promised Savior, who had come to save everybody from their sins.

Something more to think about: Jesus still helps us when we ask Him. He still heals our sicknesses and diseases. Of course, He often does His healing through other people, even through ourselves. How does Jesus let people heal us? Why is prayer to Jesus so important?

Words to help us pray: Dear Jesus, when I am sick, help me believe in Your power to make me well. When I am well, help me remember that Your power, the power of God, keeps me alive and healthy. Thank you, Jesus, for God's love and life, and everything good. Amen.

How Love Speaks Through Actions

A week before Jesus was crucified He went to Bethany, where Lazarus and his sisters lived. Lazarus was the man Jesus had brought back to life. In Bethany there also lived a man by the name of Simon, who loved Jesus very much because Jesus had cured his leprosy.

These friends of Jesus wanted to do something for Him. Simon said he would give a supper for Jesus and His friends. Martha offered to help prepare and serve the meal. Mary didn't tell what she was going to do, but she thought of something special. Lazarus just wanted to sit by Jesus.

While the men were at the table eating, Mary came in quietly with a jar of very expensive perfume. She thought it was the best gift she could give her Lord. She broke it open and poured the perfume on Jesus' head and feet. Then she knelt and wiped his feet with her long hair.

As soon as Mary did this, the sweet smell of the perfume filled the whole house. But some of the people became angry. "Why was this perfume wasted?" they said to each other.

Judas, the disciple who was going to betray Jesus, said, "This perfume could have been sold for a lot of money that we could have given to the poor!" Judas didn't really care for the poor. He wanted to steal the money for himself.

But Jesus was pleased with what Mary had done. He knew she had done this because she loved Him. He also knew that soon He would die for her. So Jesus said, "Leave Mary alone. Why are you criticizing her? She has done a beautiful thing for Me. You will always have poor people around that you can help whenever you want to. But I will not always be with you."

Jesus knew that Mary's action was her way of saying thanks for what He would soon be doing—giving up His life to save the world for God. So He said, "She poured perfume on My body to prepare it ahead of time for my burial. Remember this, what I have done will be told in the whole world. And what Mary has done for Me today will be told everywhere too."

Soon after this happened, Judas went to Jesus' enemies at the temple in Jerusalem and offered to help them capture Jesus if they would give him some money. This they gladly promised to do.

Something more to think about: How did Simon speak his love for Jesus through an action? How about Martha and Lazarus? Why was Mary's act a gift that told her love?

Florists have a motto that says, "Say it with flowers." What is the "it"? Why is a gift that speaks love never a waste?

Words that speak love:

> There is a name I love to hear;
> I love to speak its worth;
> It sounds like music in my ear,
> The sweetest name on earth.
>
> It tells me of the Savior's love,
> Who died to set me free;
> It tells me of His precious blood,
> The blood He shed for me.

The Time Jesus
Was Welcomed as a King

When Mary, the sister of Martha and Lazarus, poured costly perfume on Jesus' head and feet, she showed she knew that Jesus had chosen to die. It also showed that she loved Jesus very much.

The next day Jesus, His disciples, and a large crowd hiked to Jerusalem, a few miles away. Near Jerusalem they approached a small village at the bottom of the Mount of Olives.

"Go into that village," Jesus told two disciples. "There

you will find a donkey and a colt. Untie them and bring them to Me. If anyone tries to stop you from taking the animals, just say that the Lord needs them. Then the owner will let you have them."

The two men did what Jesus told them to do: they brought the donkey and her colt to Jesus. Then Jesus sat on the colt and began to ride into Jerusalem instead of walking as He usually did. He was showing the people that their King was coming. Some kings still parade like that.

As Jesus rode toward the city on the donkey, the crowd following Him got bigger and bigger. Some of the people ran ahead and cut branches from palm trees. These they waved like flags or threw on the ground as a welcome carpet for Jesus to ride over. Others spread their coats and robes on the road as a way of honoring Him.

When the parade reached the top of the Mount of Olives, the crowd began to thank and praise God for sending Jesus to them. "Hosanna! Hosanna!" they cheered. We would say, "Hooray to the Son of King David!" or "God bless the King, who comes in the name of the Lord!" They shouted, "Peace in heaven and glory to God!"

When some pharisees saw and heard this all, they hollered at Jesus, "Teacher, make Your disciples stop saying that!" But Jesus answered, "If they would be quiet, the stones along the way would shout."

The whole city was in an uproar when Jesus and His crowd arrived: "Who is that man who came riding into the city like a king? They're calling Him our Savior!"

The people in the crowd answered, "He is Teacher Jesus from Nazareth in Galilee." Then the worried pharisees said, "Look, the whole world is following that man."

Something more to think about: Why didn't the leaders in Jerusalem want the people to welcome Jesus and shout what they were shouting? What did Jesus mean by saying that the stones along the way would shout His praises if the people didn't? The Sunday before Easter is called Palm Sunday. Can you guess why? How can *we* welcome and praise Jesus as the Savior and King of all God's people?

Words to help us pray: Dear Jesus, You went to Jerusalem to suffer and die for us. There you saved us for eternal life with God in heaven. Be happy with our thanks, love, and praise. Rule us by being our Lord and King. Amen.

How Some Children Praised Jesus

The day Jesus rode a donkey to Jerusalem He was welcomed by large crowds along the way. They waved palm branches and shouted psalm verses: "Hosanna to the Son of David. Blessed is He who comes in the name of the Lord." They were calling Jesus the King and the Savior their God had promised to send.

Jesus was almost into Jerusalem when suddenly He

stopped. As He thought about the city, tears came to His eyes. Do you know why? He was thinking of all the people in that city who didn't believe He was their Savior.

"Oh, Jerusalem," Jesus said sadly, "if only you knew what you could have had." Then He thought of what would happen to that city in the future: "The days are coming when your enemies will surround you and smash you to the ground. Because you didn't realize that God was visiting you through Me, your children will die."

The next day Jesus and His disciples went to the temple. Again He saw all kinds of moneymaking going on. So He took some ropes and made a whip out of them. Then He drove all the animals out of the temple and tipped over the tables of the money exchangers.

When the temple was cleared and only the worshipers remained, Jesus sat down and talked to the people about God's will and ways. Many blind and lame people came to Him, and He healed them all.

In the temple some children who knew about Jesus began praising Him. "Hosanna to the Son of David," they kept shouting. "Hosanna in the highest."

When the priests and teachers of the temple came to see what all the noise was about, they said to Jesus, "Don't you hear what those children are saying? Why don't you stop them?" They were very angry because the children were calling Jesus their King and Savior.

But Jesus was pleased with the praises and the faith of the children. He said to His enemies, who didn't believe He was their Savior, "Haven't you ever read in your Scripture: 'God receives the best praise from babies and little children'?"

Then Jesus left the temple and went to Bethany, where He spent the night with friends.

Something more to think about: Why did the crowds on the street and the children in the temple cheer and praise Jesus? Why did this make the pharisees and the priests in the temple angry? What do you think makes children's praises so pleasing to God?

Words to help us sing:

> Children of the heavenly King,
> As we journey, let us sing,
> Sing our Savior's worthy praise,
> Glorious in His works and ways.

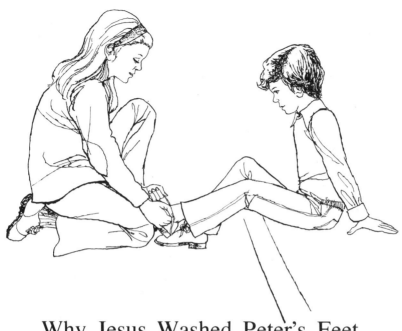

Why Jesus Washed Peter's Feet

On the day before Jesus was crucified, He knew the time had come for Him to go to His Father in heaven. Because He especially loved His closest disciples, He decided to have one last supper with them.

It was the first day of the Jewish Passover holiday, so Jesus asked His disciples to make arrangements for their Passover supper. He said to Peter and John, "Go to Jerusalem. There you will meet a man carrying a pitcher of water. Follow him, and he will take you to a large, furnished upstairs room. There get the Passover meal ready for us."

That evening Jesus and His disciples had their Passover supper together. Peter and John set the table. But there was no servant there to wash the disciples' dirty feet. People wore sandals in those days and walked on dirt streets, so their feet got pretty dirty.

Jesus decided to show His disciples something. He got up from the table, tied a towel around His waist, and poured some water into a washbowl. Then He began to wash His disciples' feet and wipe them with the towel. He was showing them how Jesus' people serve each other.

When Jesus came to Peter, Peter objected: "Are You going to wash my feet, Lord? No, I can't let You wash my feet. That's the work of a servant, and You're my master!" Jesus said to him, "You don't know yet what I'm doing, but you will later." And Peter replied, "You will never wash my feet. I won't let You."

Then Jesus said to Peter, "If I can't wash your feet, You will no longer be My disciple." The foot washing was a way of receiving Jesus' love. All people who accept Jesus' love and have their sins washed away are His disciples. After hearing that, Peter said, "Lord, not just my feet. Wash my hands and my head too."

When Jesus finished washing their feet, He put on His robe and sat down at the table again. The disciples were very quiet. They were waiting to hear what else Jesus would say.

"Do you understand what I have done?" asked Jesus. "I am your Lord and Teacher, and I have washed your feet. Now you have an example of how to love and serve one another. You do what I have done for you. Now that you know this, practice it and you will be happy."

Something more to think about: Jesus told His disciples that because He had washed them, all but one of them were completely clean. How are we completely clean because we have been washed by Jesus? Why wasn't Judas clean in his spirit? What are we to do to really enjoy being clean?

Words to help us pray: We thank You, Lord Jesus, that before dying for us You showed Your disciples how Your love makes people completely clean. Give us more of Your Holy Spirit so that we will follow Your example and serve others as You did. Amen.

The Lord's Supper

Jesus became very sad while eating a last supper with His disciples just before He died. He knew what was coming. "Soon one of you will help My enemies capture Me and kill Me," He said.

The disciples looked at one another, puzzled by what Jesus had said. Peter leaned over to John, who was sitting next to Jesus, and whispered, "Ask Him who He's talking about." So John turned to Jesus and asked, "Who is it, Lord?" Jesus answered, "The one I give a piece of bread dipped in sauce." Jesus took a piece of bread, dipped it in the sauce on the table, and gave it to Judas Iscariot.

Judas took the bread. Then Jesus said to him, "Hurry

and do what you are going to do." Judas jumped up, left the table, and hurried to tell Jesus' enemies where they could find Him.

After Judas left, Jesus took the bread from the table. Then He thanked His Father in heaven for it, broke it into pieces, and gave it to His disciples, saying, "Take it. Eat it. This is My body I'm giving for you. Do this to remember Me."

After supper Jesus filled a cup with wine. As He passed it to His disciples, He said, "All of you drink it. This is God's new promise, sealed with My blood. I am giving My blood for you for the forgiveness of your sins. Drink it as a way of remembering Me."

Jesus had the first Lord's Supper on the night He was crucified so that His disciples would understand why He was dying. He was sacrificing Himself, His body and blood, so that all people, always, everywhere, would have God's forgiveness.

After Jesus rose from the dead and went to heaven, His disciples often did as they were told. They ate some bread and drank some wine together as a way of remembering Him. And whenever they ate the bread, they thought of the time when Jesus gave His body for them by dying on the cross. And whenever they drank the wine, they remembered how Jesus had given His blood so they could have God's love, forgiveness, and life.

When they ate the bread and drank the wine, they knew they were receiving Jesus' body and blood. Today, too, people remember Jesus' wonderful gift when they

take Communion. The minister says what Jesus said when He began this sacrament: "This is My body, given for you. This is My blood, poured out for you for the forgiveness of sins."

Something more to think about: Christians believe that Jesus died so they can have God's forgiveness and love. How does the Lord's Supper help us remember that? Why is it also called Holy Communion? *Com* means *with.* With whom do we unite when we participate in Holy Communion? Jesus took for granted that His friends would repeat the Supper often. How often do you think is often?

Words to help us sing: I will sing of the love of the Lord forever. Amen.

A Command and a Promise

After Jesus showed the disciples the Lord's Supper, He talked to them a long time in that upper room. Very tenderly He said to them, "My children, I won't be with you much longer. But when I am gone, I want you to remember to love one another. Love one another just as I have loved you. If you love one another, everyone will know you are My disciples."

"Where are You going, Lord?" Simon Peter asked. Jesus answered, "Now you can't follow Me where I go, but later you can."

"Why can't I follow You now?" asked Peter. "I'm ready to die for You!" But Jesus knew that Peter really wasn't ready to die for Him. So He said, "To tell you the truth, Peter, before a rooster crows twice, you will say three times that you don't even know Me."

Then, to prepare them for the next day, Jesus gave His disciples some wonderful promises. "Don't be worried and upset," He said. "Believe in God and believe in Me. My Father has a house with many rooms, and I am going to prepare a place for you there. Really. But first I must die for you. Then I will come back and take you to where I am so that you will be with Me forever. You know where I'm going, and you know how to get there."

But Thomas, one of the 12 disciples, said to Jesus, "Lord, we don't know where You're going, so how can we know the way to get there?" Jesus answered, "I am the Way and the Truth and the Life. No one gets to the Father except by believing in Me. Now that you know Me, you also know My Father and have seen Him."

Then Philip, another disciple, said to Jesus, "Lord, show us the Father." Jesus answered, "I have been with you all this time, and you still don't know Me, Philip? If you've seen Me, you've seen the Father. So why do you say, 'Show us the Father'? Believe Me, I am in the Father, and the Father is in Me." Jesus also told the disciples that the Father's glory would be seen in Him and in the works His followers would do.

To help them carry on His work, Jesus promised His disciples a Helper. They would not be left alone. He told them, "If you love Me, you will obey My commandments. And I will ask the Father to give you another Helper, the Holy Spirit, who will stay with you forever. The Holy Spirit will continue My work by teaching you and reminding you of all that I said."

Something more to think about: What was the parting command Jesus wanted His followers to obey more than any other? Why do Christians believe that the only way to know God is to get to know Jesus? Why did Jesus promise to give the Holy Spirit to His disciples?

Words to help us pray: Lord Jesus, You are the way to God and life with Him in heaven. God the Father was in You and all that You said and did. Give us the Holy Spirit to help us do Your will and works. Especially help us love one another. Amen.

Prayers Jesus Prayed

On the night before Jesus died, He prayed for His followers: "Father, I showed You to the men You gave Me. I gave them Your message. They know I came from You. Now I pray for them. Holy Father, by Your power keep them safe. Then they will be one just as You and I are one."

Jesus also said, "I pray for all who will believe in Me through the disciples' message. Father, let them all be one. Keep them in Us just as We are in each other. Let them be one just as We are one. I will be in them and You in Me. Then the world will know that You love them as You love Me."

After praying, Jesus took a walk with His disciples to a garden called Gethsemane. At the gate of the garden Jesus said to them, "Wait here while I go to pray." Then He took Peter, James, and John into the garden. "You three stay here and watch with Me," He said. "I feel very, very sad."

Jesus went a little farther into the garden by Himself, threw Himself down on the ground, and talked to His Father in heaven: "Father, if it is possible, take this suffering away from Me. But don't do what I want. Let Your will be done."

When Jesus returned to the three disciples, He found them sound asleep. They didn't appreciate what their Lord was suffering for them! And how sad it must have made Jesus. Even His closest friends didn't realize what He was facing. He woke them and said, "Why can't you three watch with Me for even an hour? Watch and pray so you don't fall into temptation."

Jesus went away and prayed again. When He returned, He found the same thing: there they were, asleep. So He went away once more to pray. And while He was praying, an angel came to Him from heaven to tell Him something. His Father in heaven would help Him go through with God's plan for saving the world.

Now Jesus felt strong enough to die for us. So He returned to the three disciples. . . . And found them fast asleep. Then He woke them and said, "It's time for us to go." You see, His disciple Judas was coming with some soldiers to capture Him.

Jesus knew He was about to be crucified for saying He was the Son of God and the Savior of the world. He was willing to die to save the world. And by praying, He got the strength He needed.

Something more to think about: Why did Jesus want His followers to be one? What do you think it means to belong to Jesus' one big happy family? Why did Jesus pray in the Garden of Gethsemane? What did He pray three times? How will praying help us when we have a difficult problem or task?

Words to help us remember Jesus:
>Go to dark Gethsemane,
>You who feel the Tempter's power;
>Your Redeemer's conflict see,
>Watch with Him one bitter hour.
>Turn not from His griefs away;
>Learn from Jesus Christ to pray.

The Way Jesus Fought for Us

Some kids think of John Wayne as a big hero because he acted tough in a lot of pictures. Some people think their leaders are stronger when they give orders and lay down the law. But sometimes it takes more faith and more strength not to fight than to fight.

As Jesus was talking to His three sleepy friends in the Garden of Gethsemane, a group of soldiers from the Temple Guard arrived. They had been sent by the priests and officers of the temple to capture Jesus. Judas, one of

Jesus' disciples, was leading the soldiers and a large crowd that had followed them.

Judas had told the soldiers, "The man I kiss is the man you want. Grab Him and arrest Him." When Judas arrived, he went straight to Jesus and greeted Him with a kiss, the way some people still welcome each other. But Jesus looked sadly at Judas and said, "Judas, are you betraying Me with a kiss?"

Then, instead of trying to run away, Jesus turned to the soldiers and asked, "Whom are you looking for?" As if He didn't know! They answered, "Jesus of Nazareth."

"I am He," Jesus said. The startled soldiers stepped back. Some fell to the ground. Jesus asked again, "For whom are you looking?" Again they said, "Jesus of Nazareth." Jesus replied, "I've already told you, I am He. If you are looking for Me, let these others go."

But one of the disciples (you could guess it was Peter) shouted, "Lord, shall we fight them with our swords?" Then he pulled out his sword, charged, and cut off a man's ear. But Jesus said to Peter, "Put your sword away. All who use the sword will die by the sword. Don't you know that I could call on My Father for help, and He would immediately send Me more than 12 armies of angels?"

Then Jesus showed the love and power of God by touching the man's ear and healing it. After this the soldiers grabbed Jesus, tied His hands behind Him, and took Him away to jail. All His disciples left Him and ran away.

Something more to think about: Why didn't Jesus arm His followers and fight to become the king of the Jews? Why didn't He run away and escape while He had the chance? What did Jesus believe about the power of God? Why didn't the power of God save Jesus? In what ways is it still true that those who use force are destroyed by force?

Words to help us pray: We thank You, dear Savior, that You allowed Yourself to be captured so that Your followers could all be free of fear and the devil's powers. Keep us from ever thinking we have to fight God's battles with physical force or violence. Give us the love and peace of Jesus at all times. Amen.

It Wasn't a Fair Trial

The priests and leaders of the people in Jerusalem hated Jesus. They were afraid He was becoming too popular and powerful, and they didn't want His kind of kingdom.

So they sent soldiers led by Judas, Jesus' disciple, and captured Jesus in the Garden of Gethsemane. They brought Jesus to a house in Jerusalem for questioning. It was the house of Annas, the father-in-law of Jerusalem's head priest.

Annas asked Jesus about His teachings and His disciples. He didn't really want to know; he was just looking for something he could use against Jesus.

"I have always spoken openly," Jesus answered. "I have taught in the schools and in the temple, and I've taught nothing secretly. Why do you question Me? Ask the people who heard Me. They know what I said."

Then one of the guards standing by Jesus slapped Him in the face and said, "How dare you talk like that to a high priest?" This didn't frighten Jesus one bit. "If I've said anything wrong, tell everyone here what it was," He said. "But if I said right, why did you hit Me?"

Annas decided to send Jesus to Caiaphas [Kay-ah-fuss], the chief Jewish ruler in the city. A meeting of the city council had been called, and the leaders were gathering at Caiaphas's house.

When the council members were all seated, the guard brought Jesus to them for a trial. They all tried to find some evidence against Jesus so they would have a reason for putting Him to death. But the many people who came and told lies about Jesus couldn't even agree with each other.

Finally two men stepped up and said, "This man said, 'Tear down this temple, and I will raise it back up in 3 days.'" By *temple* Jesus meant His body, but the witnesses made it sound like He had spoken about the temple buildings. Then Caiaphas stood up and said to Jesus, "What's Your answer to this charge?" Jesus remained silent. Caiaphas said, "In the name of the living God, I now put You under oath. Tell us if You are the Messiah, the Son of God."

To this Jesus said, "If I tell you, you will not believe Me or let Me go. But the next time you see me, I will be sitting at the right side of God and coming from the clouds of heaven." Then all the leaders shouted, "Are You saying You're the Son of God?"

Jesus answered, "I am."

Then the high priest, Caiaphas, tore his robes in anger. "We don't need any more witnesses," he said. "What do you all think?" And they all shouted, "He is guilty and must die."

Something more to think about: Why didn't Jesus get a fair trial? What wasn't fair about it? Why wasn't Jesus one bit afraid to speak? Why did He sometimes not answer? The Bible says that Jesus suffered so we could have

life with God. How can Jesus help us when unfriendly people don't listen to us?

Words to help us pray: Thank You, Jesus, for allowing sinful, unfair people to put You on trial. Thank You for suffering to save us and the world from such evil. By Your love keep us from treating other people unfairly. Amen.

Nothing to Crow About

Bragging is sometimes called crowing, the sound a rooster makes. When Jesus told His disciples that they would all run away and leave Him, Peter spoke up and said to Jesus, "I'll never leave You, even if the rest do!" Then Jesus said to Peter, "Remember this! Before a rooster crows twice tonight, you will say three times that you don't know Me." Peter was sure this couldn't happen, so he said, "I will never do that, even if I have to die with You."

Later Peter followed the enemies of Jesus when they captured Him and took Him to the house of Annas. While Jesus was on trial in the house of Caiaphas, Peter hung around the palace courtyard to see what would happen.

The night was cold, and the soldiers who were on duty outside made a fire. As they stood around the fire warming themselves, they talked about Jesus and what was happening. Because Peter was cold too, he joined them and listened to what they were saying. Then one of the maids saw Peter's face, lit by the fire. "You were with this Jesus," she said.

That frightened Peter. "I don't know what you're talking about," he said. As he walked away, a rooster crowed. Then another maid by the fire said to the men there, "I know he was with this Jesus of Nazareth." Again Peter denied it: "I swear, I don't know that man." So some of the men who had been standing at the fire went over and said to him, "Don't try to fool us. Of course you're one of Jesus' followers. Your accent gives you away."

Then Peter panicked. He began to curse and swear. He said, "May God punish me if I'm not telling the truth.

I do not know the man you are talking about!" Just then a rooster in the yard crowed a second time. Startled by what he heard, Peter looked up and saw Jesus being taken from the council room to a guard room. Jesus just looked at Peter. He knew what Peter had said.

Oh, how bad Peter suddenly felt. Now he realized

what he had done. And he thought he would never deny knowing Jesus! Peter was very sorry. He ran out of the yard and cried and cried.

Peter could never crow about what he did. But what he did was something we can all easily do. Even though we are Jesus' followers, we often hide that from people. This makes Jesus sad. Remembering the loving look Jesus gave Peter ought to make us sorry too.

Something more to think about: How do we sometimes say we don't know Jesus? What might be some of our reasons? How can we be sure that Jesus forgives us even when we desert Him? What happens to us when we realize how much Jesus loves us?

Words to help us pray: Help us, dear Jesus. We can't always remain loyal to You without Your help. Keep us from pretending we don't know You and don't love You. And if we do pretend, make us sorry by Your look of love and forgiveness. Amen.

King Jesus, Our King

The city council met in the house of Caiaphas and decided that Jesus had to be put to death. But they weren't permitted to kill anyone. The Romans ruled the people of Jerusalem. The Roman governor made such final decisions. So early on the day that Jesus was crucified, the Jewish leaders took Jesus to Pontius Pilate, the Roman governor.

Jesus' enemies wanted to see Him hanging on a cross. That was how they killed criminals in those days. When Pilate asked the Jewish leaders their reasons for wanting Jesus dead, they said, "We caught Him misleading our people. He told them not to pay taxes, and then He claimed He is the Christ, a king."

Pilate thought he'd better investigate these charges. He took Jesus into his palace and asked, "Are You the king of the Jews?" Jesus answered, "I am a king. But My kingdom is not like the kingdoms of this world. If it were, My followers would fight to keep Me from being captured."

"Are You a king then?" Pilate asked. "Whatever you say!" Jesus answered. "I came into the world to speak the truth. Whoever loves the truth listens to Me."

"What is truth?" asked Pilate.

While Pilate was talking to Jesus, a servant came in. He bowed and handed Pilate a message from his wife. It said, "Don't have anything to do with this innocent man. I had a bad dream about Him last night."

Then Pilate went out to the front of his palace, where the enemies of Jesus were waiting. "I can't find anything wrong with Jesus," he told them. But they shouted, "He and His teachings are starting trouble all over our country. He began in Galilee, and now He has come here."

When Pilate heard that Jesus had lived in Galilee, he sent Jesus to another king, Herod, who was in Jerusalem at the time. Herod was the ruler of Galilee. Herod was pleased when the guards brought Jesus to him. He had been wanting to see Jesus perform a miracle.

Herod asked Jesus many questions, but Jesus wouldn't say a word. He just stood there. Then when the priests and the Bible teachers accused Jesus of all sorts of things, Herod decided it was all a big joke. He made fun of Jesus. His servants put a white robe on Him. Some dangerous king that Jesus was! Then after his joke, Herod sent Jesus back to Pilate.

Something more to think about: Why wasn't Pilate worried when he heard that Jesus was a king? What kind of people did Jesus say He ruled? Why wouldn't Jesus say

a word to King Herod? If you had to choose between a king like Herod and King Jesus, why would you choose Jesus? How does King Jesus rule His people?

A song about King Jesus:

Hark! The herald angels sing,
"Glory to the King of kings;
Peace on earth and mercy mild,
God and sinners reconciled!"
Hark! The herald angels sing,
"Glory to the King of kings."

A Man Who Couldn't Clean His Hands

When King Herod sent Jesus back to Pontius Pilate, Pilate tried reasoning with the crowd outside his palace: "I have examined this man. He is not guilty of any of the crimes you say He did. He has done nothing wrong. He doesn't deserve to die. Because He is innocent, I will have Him whipped and let Him go."

This made the enemies of Jesus angry at Pilate. They began to yell at him. Pilate started worrying. Maybe he'd get into trouble if he didn't do what they wanted. Then he got a bright idea.

He said to the crowd, "Every year during your Passover celebration I set a prisoner free for you. Who should I set free, Jesus the King of the Jews or Barabbas?" Because Barabbas was a murderer, Pilate was sure the people would choose Jesus. They were afraid of Barabbas.

But the priests got the crowd to ask for Barabbas instead of Jesus. "Give us Barabbas! Give us Barabbas! Not this man! We want Barabbas!" they chanted. "What do you want me to do with your King of the Jews?" Pilate asked. "Nail Him to a cross! Crucify Him!" they all shouted.

"Why? What crime has He done?" asked Pilate. They didn't care. "Crucify Him. Crucify Him!" they shouted all the louder. "But I can't find anything wrong with Him," Pilate said. "*You* take Him and crucify Him."

"We have a law," said the priests. "And by our law He deserves to die. He called Himself the Son of God."

Pilate thought a riot might start. He called for a bowl of water and washed his hands in front of the mob. "I'm not responsible for the death of this man! That will be *your* doing," he said. They shouted back, "Right! We'll take His blood on us and on our children!" They were saying that they'd accept the blame for Jesus' death. Because Pilate wanted to please the mob, he set Barabbas free. Then he ordered his soldiers to whip Jesus and hang Him on a cross.

Pilate's soldiers and their buddies dragged Jesus into the yard of the palace. They put a purple robe on Jesus, made a crown out of sharp, thorny branches, and jammed it on His head. Then they started making fun of Jesus. They saluted Him and said, "Long live the King of the Jews!" Then they hit Him on the head with a stick, spit in His face, and bowed down to Him. When they had finished making fun of Him, they put His clothes back on and led Him away to be crucified.

Something more to think about: By washing His hands in front of the mob, Pilate was saying that he wasn't crucifying Jesus; they were. Why didn't that action give him a clean record or make him innocent? What should Pilate have done when he was convinced that Jesus was innocent? The Bible says, "The person who doesn't do the good he knows he should do is guilty of sin" (James 4:17). How do we sometimes act innocent or holy when we're not? But, remember, Jesus suffered and died for those sins too.

Words to help us pray: Dear Father in heaven, help us appreciate how much Jesus had to suffer to take away the sins of the world. For His sake forgive us our sins, especially our sins of pretending we're innocent when we're not. Amen.

How Cruel People Can Be

You want to know how cruel people can be? Read what they did to Jesus just before He died. Nobody ever suffered more mean treatment than He suffered.

First, when they captured Him in the Garden of Gethsemane, they beat Him for no good reason. They made fun of Him. They blindfolded Him and asked Him to tell who hit Him.

Next came the unfair trial before the city council. Witnesses told lies about Him. The jury looked for an excuse to kill Him.

Pontius Pilate, the Roman governor, tried to free Jesus. He knew that Jesus was innocent of any crime. But he was afraid to do what was right. So he sent Jesus to Herod, the ruler of Galilee. Herod and his soldiers made fun of Jesus. They sent Him back to Pilate in a white robe.

Even though Pilate washed his hands and acted innocent, he ordered his soldiers to whip and crucify Jesus just to please the crowd. That very morning, with His back ripped open and His head bleeding from a crown made out of thorny branches, Jesus had to carry a big wooden cross from Pilate's court to Mount Calvary.

The hill where Jesus was crucified was about a mile away. The road Jesus walked to get there is now called the Way of Sorrows. Worn out from no rest and terrible beatings, Jesus fell down when He tried to carry the big cross by Himself.

Some women who saw how Jesus was suffering felt sorry for Him and cried. But Jesus looked at them and said, "Don't cry for Me; cry for yourselves and your children." He wanted them to be sorry for all the sins that were causing Him to suffer and die.

When Jesus couldn't move fast enough for the soldiers, they grabbed an African named Simon of Cyrene, who was visiting the city. They made him carry Jesus' cross.

Jesus had often said that people could not be His disciples unless they were willing to carry His cross. He meant that His disciples must be willing to suffer with Him.

When the crowd reached the place called Golgotha, the soldiers took off Jesus' clothes and tied a short apron around Him. Then they laid Him against the big wooden cross and pounded nails through His hands and feet. Next they lifted up the cross with Jesus hanging on it and stuck it in a hole to hold it in place.

Something more to think about: Why are people often cruel? Can you think of a time when you were mean to somebody? What was your reason? The Bible says that

Jesus suffered for us in order to take away our sins. It also says that we should follow in His footsteps. How might our willingness to suffer help take away some sins of other people?

A song that praises Jesus:

> Glory be to Jesus,
> Who in bitter pains
> Poured for me the lifeblood
> From His sacred veins!
>
> Grace and life eternal
> In that blood I find;
> Blest be His compassion
> Infinitely kind!

What All Happened When Jesus Died

Ever wonder why the day Jesus died is called *Good* Friday? What was good about it? Can anyone's death ever be good?

At 9 o'clock in the morning Jesus was nailed to a cross. Two other men were crucified with Him, one on each side of Him. The first thing Jesus said from the cross was: "Father, forgive them; they don't know what they're doing."

Jesus hung there 6 hours before He died. He was

suffering to take away the sins of the world, not for any wrong He had done. But many people came to watch Him and make fun of Him. They laughed and shouted, "He saved others, but He cannot save Himself." Some of them said, "If You are the Son of God, come on down from the cross."

Even one of the robbers who was being crucified began to yell at Jesus. "If You are the Savior, save Yourself and us." But the other robber believed that Jesus was God's Son. He believed Jesus was suffering innocently for other people's sins.

So he said to the other robber, "Aren't you afraid of God? We are guilty and are getting what we deserve for what we did. But Jesus did nothing wrong." Then he turned to Jesus and said, "Lord, remember me when You become king." Jesus turned to the robber who believed in Him and said, "Today you will be in heaven with Me."

By His life and death Jesus opened the doors of heaven for all who believe. Jesus won for us forgiveness of all sin and a perfect life in paradise forever. As soon as we die, we go to live with God. That's why the day Jesus died is called Good Friday, a very good day to remember.

Suddenly at noon the sun disappeared. For 3 whole hours it was dark as night. God was sad. Once, in the darkness, Jesus shouted, "My God, My God, why have You left Me?" Jesus suffered separation from God so that *we* would never have to feel separated from God's love.

About 3 o'clock in the afternoon Jesus said, "It is finished!" His work of saving people from their sins was done. He spoke quietly once more: "Father, into Your hands I place My spirit." Then He died.

At once the ground began to shake. Huge boulders broke open. A large curtain in the temple ripped in half from top to bottom. And the army captain who saw what was happening said, "This man certainly was the Son of God."

Something more to think about: Now can you answer the questions that were asked at the beginning? Do you understand why Christians call the day Jesus died a good day? What was good about it? Even though we are sad about losing the person, why can we be happy when a Christian dies?

Words to help us pray: Lord Jesus, our Savior and King, we praise and thank You that through Your suffering and death You opened the doors of heaven for us. Keep our eyes always on You. Then we too will serve God and enter Your heavenly kingdom. Amen.

The Happiest Day of the Year

Which do you think is the happiest day of the year? Many people would say Christmas, their birthday, or the day they were married. Good Friday is a good day because of the blessings that keep coming from the death of Jesus, but Good Friday is not a happy day. No, the happiest day

of the year for the followers of Jesus is Easter. Here's why:

The night Jesus died, two of His friends went to Pilate and asked for permission to bury His body. Pilate let them. So they lovingly took Jesus' body off the cross and wrapped it in clean, white cloth. Then they carried it to a nearby garden and laid it in a grave cut out of the side of a hill. It was like a cave.

After putting Jesus in the grave, they rolled a big stone in front of the entrance. Some of the women friends of Jesus watched as He was buried and then left.

Jesus' enemies also talked to Pilate. They asked him

to seal the grave and have soldiers guard it. They were afraid the disciples of Jesus might try to steal the body.

Because the next day was the Sabbath, not much happened. In the Old Testament God had told His people to rest on Saturday.

But early Sunday morning some women went to the garden where Jesus had been buried. They showed their love by bringing sweet spices to put around Jesus' body. But they wondered how they could roll away the stone from the entrance of the grave.

When they came to the grave, they found the stone already rolled away from the door. Surprised, they tiptoed into the grave, but Jesus' body wasn't there. What could have happened? Then two men in bright clothes appeared. "Why are you looking in a tomb for one who is alive? Jesus is not here. He is risen. Go and tell His friends," said God's messengers.

Then the women remembered. Jesus had said He would become alive again on the third day. So back they hurried to Jerusalem to tell the other disciples what they had seen and heard. Imagine how they must have felt!

Something more to think about: Now you know the happiest day of the year for Christians. It's the day they say to one another, "Happy Easter! Jesus is alive!" But why are Jesus' followers so happy He became alive again? What are some of the reasons?

A happy Easter song:

I know that my Redeemer lives;
What comfort this sweet sentence gives!

He lives, He lives, who once was dead;
He lives, my everliving Head.

He lives to bless me with His love,
He lives to plead for me above,
He lives my hungry soul to feed,
He lives to help in time of need.

He lives to silence all my fears,
He lives to wipe away my tears,
He lives to calm my troubled heart,
He lives all blessings to impart.

Times When Jesus Appeared

On the first Easter day some women who loved Jesus went to visit His grave and found it was open. What a surprise! Mary Magdalene ran back to the city to tell Peter and John what she had seen. But the other women first went into the cave and looked for Jesus' body.

Then they went back to tell the disciples what had happened. And Mary Magdalene returned to the garden. First she stood outside the grave and cried. She thought Jesus' enemies must have taken His body away.

After a while she peeked into the tomb and saw two angels sitting where Jesus' body had been. "Woman, why are you crying?" they asked her. "They have taken away my Lord, and I don't know where they put Him," she answered.

Then she turned around. There was Jesus standing behind her. But she didn't know it was Jesus. "Woman, why are you crying? Whom are you looking for?" Jesus asked. "Sir, if you took Him away, please tell me where you put Him," Mary said. She thought Jesus was the gardener. Jesus said to her, "Mary!"

When Mary heard her name spoken so lovingly, she knew. It was Jesus! *"Rabboni!"* she said to Him in Hebrew. That means "teacher." She was so happy that she wanted to hug Him. But Jesus said, "Don't try to hug Me, Mary. Go and tell My brothers that I am going back to My Father and your Father, My God and your God." So Mary went and told the disciples that she had seen Jesus alive.

Next Jesus appeared to the other women, who were on their way to the disciples. When He greeted them, they recognized Him. "Don't be afraid," He said to them. "Go tell My brothers to go to Galilee. There they will see Me."

That same day two disciples of Jesus were walking to Emmaus, a small town near Jerusalem, when a man joined them. "What are you talking about?" He asked. "Why are you so sad?" The disciple Cleopas said, "Boy, are you a stranger here! Don't you know what has happened in Jerusalem?"

"What?" the stranger asked.

Then Cleopas told the stranger about Jesus. "You

foolish men," said Jesus. "Why don't you believe what the prophets said? The Savior had to suffer and die. That's why he came here." Then Jesus explained to them what the Old Testament said about Him.

At last they came to the village where the two men lived. Jesus acted as though He were going farther. But they said to Him, "Stay with us. The day is almost over, and it's getting dark." So Jesus went with them into their house. At the supper He took the loaf of bread that was on the table, broke off some of it, and gave it to them, just like He used to. Suddenly they recognized Him. Then He disappeared.

Something more to think about: Why do people who

love someone very much often visit the loved person's grave? Christians say, "I believe in the resurrection of the body." Why do we believe that God's children live with Jesus after they die? How does this wipe away tears?

Words to help us pray: Risen and loving Savior, we're glad You showed Yourself alive to Mary, then to the two disciples in Emmaus. Stay with us in our homes and help us see that You are with us always. Amen.

No Reason to Doubt

Two disciples who thought Jesus was dead discovered Him alive in their home. Off they hurried, back to Jerusalem, to tell the other disciples the news. There they found Jesus' followers meeting in a house. Everyone was excited. "The Lord is alive and appeared to Simon," the men from Emmaus were told. Then they got to tell about what had just happened to them.

While they were still talking, Jesus suddenly appeared in the room. Were they all scared! They thought they were seeing a ghost. But Jesus calmed them: "Don't be so upset and doubting. Look at My hands and feet. See, it's really Me. If I were a ghost, I wouldn't have flesh and bones, would I."

Then Jesus showed them His hands and feet. But they still couldn't believe He was really alive again. "Do you have anything to eat here?" He asked. When they gave Him a piece of cooked fish and He ate it, they all knew Jesus was really alive. But now His body could be everywhere always.

Now Jesus told them what they would be doing. "You must tell the message of repentance and forgiveness everywhere. Later I will help you by giving you the power My Father promised. But until then you must wait here. Just as My Father sent Me, now I am sending You," He said.

That first Easter evening all 11 disciples were present except Thomas. We don't know where he was, but he may have given up his dreams about Jesus. So some of the other disciples ran to Thomas. "We saw Jesus alive," they shouted with joy. Thomas shook his head, "Oh, no. I won't believe that till I can put my fingers on the nail holes in His hands and touch the cut on His side."

A week later the disciples were meeting again in Jerusalem. This time Thomas was present. The doors were locked. But suddenly Jesus was standing there with them. "Peace to all of you," He said. Then He said to Thomas, "Put your finger here. Touch My hands. Feel the cut in My side. And then stop your doubting and believe."

When Thomas saw it was really Jesus talking to him, he shouted, "My Lord and my God!" He no longer doubted that Jesus was alive. But Jesus said, "Thomas, do you believe just because you see Me? Those who believe without seeing Me are more blessed."

Something more to think about: In what ways are we better off by not seeing Jesus in any one place? How can we be sure that Jesus is alive? What blessings does Jesus give to all who believe in Him?

Words to help us pray: Forgive us, Lord, when we forget or doubt that You are the living Son of God and our Lord and Savior. By Your Word and Spirit keep our faith strong so that we will always enjoy Your love. Amen.

What Jesus Told Peter to Do

Peter just couldn't forget what he had done. He had pretended he didn't know Jesus, even though he said he would die for Jesus. Now Jesus was alive again. Would He forgive Peter and let him be one of His workers?

Jesus had told His friends He would meet them again in Galilee. So Peter and six other disciples went up there to a big lake. Peter was nervous and didn't know what to do with himself. "I'm going fishing," he said. "We'll all go," the rest added. So they got into a boat and went out on the lake. But all that night they didn't even catch one fish.

Morning came. As they rowed back to the shore in their empty boat, they saw a man standing there. "Did you catch any fish?" the man yelled. "No," shouted Peter, "we didn't catch a thing."

"Then throw your net out on the right side of the boat," the man shouted back. Ha! What good would that do? But they tried it anyway, and their net was filled with fish. It was so full, they couldn't even pull it in.

When John saw the net full of fish, he remembered two other times when this had happened. So he turned to Peter and whispered, "It's the Lord!" Peter grabbed his robe, jumped into the lake, and waded to the shore as fast as he could go. The others followed in the boat, dragging the net full of fish behind them.

On shore they saw some fish roasting on a fire. "Bring some of those you caught," said the man. So Peter went and pulled the net full of fish to the shore. But no one dared ask the man who He was, even though they all knew it must be the Lord Jesus. "Come, let's eat together," said Jesus. And they did.

After breakfast Jesus stood up and went over to Peter. "Simon," He said, "do you really love Me? More than these others do?" Peter could hardly answer. He knew why Jesus was asking him that question. "Yes, Lord," said Peter sheepishly. "You know I love You." Jesus looked at him for quite a while and then said, "All right. Feed My lambs." Peter was to prove his love by teaching children for Jesus.

But now Peter could hardly believe that Jesus was still willing to have him as a helper. So Jesus asked Peter a second time, "Do you really love Me, Simon?" Peter answered again, "Yes, Lord, You know I love You." This time Jesus said, "Well, then also feed My sheep."

To impress on Peter that words and promises alone are not enough, Jesus asked him a third time, "Simon, do you love Me?" Now Peter felt sad that Jesus had asked him again. Almost in tears, Peter said, "Lord, You know everything. You know I love You."

"Feed My sheep" was all that Jesus said.

Something more to think about: Who are the lambs and sheep of Jesus, the Good Shepherd? What are they to be fed? Who feeds Jesus' lambs and sheep? How can teaching for Jesus be one of the best ways to love Him? Why does everyone who really loves Jesus teach others about Him and His Gospel?

Words to help us pray: Lord Jesus, You know we love You. Make us willing to feed Your lambs and sheep the Good News of God's love. Amen.

Where Jesus Is Now

For 40 days after His death Jesus appeared to His disciples many times. Usually He talked to them about the kingdom of God.

For one of these meetings Jesus told His disciples to go back to Galilee, where He had spent most of His life. He said He would meet them there on a special hill.

When they all arrived there, Jesus said to them: "Full power has been given to Me in heaven and on earth. Now go to all people everywhere and make them My disciples. Baptize them in the name of the Father, the Son, and the Holy Spirit. Teach them to do everything I have commanded you. And remember, I will always be with you."

This was the great mission command Jesus gave His followers. It's our command too. We are to make disciples for Jesus by baptizing and teaching people to believe and do all that He taught. And we know that Jesus is always with us, helping us in our work for Him.

Some of the disciples may have thought that Jesus would live there with them as He had before His death. At their last meal together one of them had asked Jesus, "Lord, will Your kingdom now come to the people of Israel?"

"Nobody knows that but God," Jesus had answered.

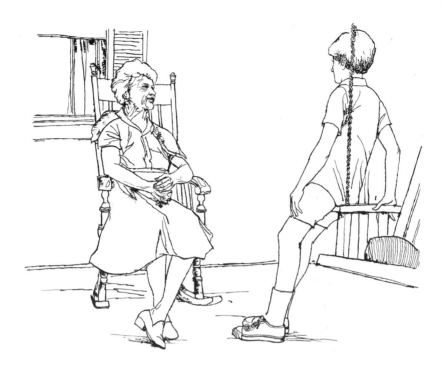

"Don't worry about it. But you will receive power when the Holy Spirit comes to you. Then you will speak for Me, telling people in Jerusalem and all over the world about life in My kingdom."

After dinner Jesus took His disciples up the Mount of Olives, a hill just outside Jerusalem. They climbed to the top. Then He told them to wait for the next few days in Jerusalem until He sent them the Holy Spirit. Next He raised His hands and blessed them. As He did so, a white cloud came along and Jesus disappeared into heaven.

There the disciples stood, staring at the cloud, when two men dressed in white suddenly appeared. "Why are you fellows standing here looking up at the sky?" they said. "Jesus was taken into heaven, but He will come back in the same way you saw Him go."

So the disciples returned to Jerusalem. They were very happy. They would no longer see Jesus, but they knew He was alive and with them. So every day they met with the other friends of Jesus and praised God and prayed for the Spirit Jesus had promised to give them.

Something more to think about: When Jesus was killed, His followers were afraid they would not be able to carry on His work. Why did they feel weak and afraid? What power did Jesus promise to give them? How can we get the power of Jesus?

Words to help us pray: Lord Jesus, King of heaven and earth, we're happy that You ascended into heaven. We know Your glory is above all things. Rule us and give us Your power, Jesus. Give us the Holy Spirit. Amen.

The Birthday of Our Lord's Church

Just before Jesus went into heaven, He promised that God would send the Holy Spirit to His disciples. The Holy Spirit, He said, would help them understand what He had taught them. The Spirit also would help them do what He wanted them to do.

So for 10 days the disciples of Jesus stayed in Jerusalem. They were waiting for God's Spirit. Every day they met together in a large house and prayed and studied their Bible.

On the tenth day after Jesus went into heaven there was a big celebration in Jerusalem. It was the day called Pentecost, a day like Thanksgiving Day. The city was full of Jews from all over the world. They had come to their temple to praise and thank God for their harvests.

Suddenly there was a noise that sounded like a very strong wind. It came from the sky, like a tornado, and went into the house where the disciples of Jesus were meeting. Then what looked like little flames of fire appeared above everyone's head.

When the people in the city heard the noise of the wind, a big crowd gathered at the place where the sound had gone. There the people got excited. They were from all over the world, but they were hearing the disciples talking in the languages of their home countries.

Surprised at this, the people said, "These men are all from Galilee. How can it be that we hear them speaking in our own language? What does this mean?" Some made fun of the disciples by saying, "These men are drunk!"

Then Peter stood up. No longer was he afraid to speak for Jesus. He said to the crowd: "Fellow Jews, listen to me. I will tell you what this all means. We aren't drunk. This is what the prophet Joel said God would do. He would send His Spirit, and all who asked God's help would be saved.

"You people of Israel killed Jesus by letting sinful

men nail Him to a cross. But God raised Him from the dead, and we are all witnesses to this. Now God has taken Jesus to heaven, where He rules for His heavenly Father."

This frightened the people. They said to Peter, "What shall we do?" Peter answered, "Turn away from your sins and be baptized, every one of you. Then your sins will be forgiven, and you too will receive God's gift, the Holy Spirit."

That day about 3,000 people believed Peter's message and were baptized. They too received the Holy Spirit and became Jesus' disciples. That was the beginning of the Christian church, the church of our Lord Jesus Christ.

Something more to think about: Why is Pentecost called the birthday of our Lord's church? What did the Holy Spirit do for those first Christians in Jerusalem? How did the people who weren't believers receive the Holy Spirit and faith in Jesus? How does the church of Jesus continue to grow?

Words that praise God:

> Let songs of praises fill the sky:
> Christ our ascended Lord
> Sends down His Spirit from on high
> According to His Word.
> All hail the day of Pentecost,
> The coming of the Holy Ghost.

The First Church of Jesus Christ

Do you still remember what happened on that Pentecost day, 10 days after Jesus disappeared into heaven? Peter told the people they had killed Jesus by letting wicked men crucify Him. "But," Peter said, "God raised Jesus from the dead and made Him our Lord and Savior, who now rules God's kingdom and people."

That Pentecost day about 3,000 people were baptized and joined the little group of about 120 followers of Jesus in that city. At first these believers met together every day to learn more about Jesus and His teachings. They ate together and prayed together.

As they preached everywhere in Jerusalem, God added more and more people to His church. These first believers had a wonderful spirit. They were thankful for what Jesus had done for them, and they were happy to have God's forgiveness and love. They loved God by loving each other.

Here are some of the things they did for one another: They shared everything they owned. Those who had money helped those who were poor. They ate together in their homes and shared their food. Some Christians even sold their land and houses and gave the money to the disciples who were their leaders. No one said that any of his belongings was his own.

So at first Jesus' followers lived together happily, loving and helping one another. They talked to each other about Jesus' being alive and always with them, even though they could no longer see Him. They celebrated His special supper whenever they met together. That was to help them remember how much He loved them and how He had died to save them from their sins.

When other people saw how kind and good Jesus' followers were, they became believers in Jesus too. Soon there were so many people in that first church in Jerusalem that the ministers couldn't take care of them all.

So they told everyone in the church to come to a meeting. They said, "We can't do all the work and the preaching and teaching of God's Word too. We need helpers to visit the sick and take care of the widows, orphans, and poor people." The group then picked seven men to help the leaders.

One helper was a young man named Stephen. The Bible says he was "full of faith and the Holy Spirit." He worked hard for Jesus. He helped with the church work and told people about the love of Jesus. And so the church in Jerusalem grew.

Something more to think about: How do people get the Holy Spirit? When people get the Holy Spirit, what do they do? What made the first church in Jerusalem grow? Have you thought about becoming a worker for the church of Jesus Christ?

Words to help us pray: Lord Jesus, thank You for making us members of Your church and giving us Your love and Holy Spirit. Also give us a willingness to serve You by loving and helping others. Amen.

How Philip Worked for Jesus

One of the seven chosen to do the church's work in Jerusalem was a young man named Philip. One day an angel of God spoke to Philip: "Go down to the road that runs from Jerusalem to Gaza."

That must have seemed like a strange message. What was he to do on that road? He wasn't likely to meet anyone there, especially at the hottest time of the day. But Philip did what he thought God wanted him to do.

As he walked down that lonely road, Philip heard the rattle of some wheels behind him. Looking back, he saw a beautiful carriage coming. In the front sat a coachman, driving some extra fine horses Behind him, under a sunshade, sat a black man reading a scroll. Philip stood to one side to let the horses go by.

When the carriage passed him, Philip saw that the man who was reading was an important official from Ethiopia, a country in Africa. He was the treasurer of his country but had been visiting Jerusalem. He was interested in the God and religion of the Jews and was returning home after worshiping in the temple.

The Holy Spirit said to Philip, "Stay close to that carriage." So Philip ran up to it and asked the man, "Do you understand what you're reading?" The man replied, "I need someone to explain it to me." He invited Philip to climb up and sit with him and showed Philip the scroll.

The man had been reading a part of the 53d chapter of the book of Isaiah in the Old Testament. It speaks about the Savior, the Lamb of God who would suffer silently as He was being mistreated and killed.

He said to Philip, "Tell me, is the prophet saying this about himself or about someone else?" Now Philip knew why he had been sent by God to that place. It was a chance for him to tell the man about Jesus. So he told him how

Jesus had suffered and died on a cross to take away everyone's sins. He also told how Jesus had become alive again and was now with God, ruling God's kingdom and church.

As they traveled down the road, they came to a place where there was some water. The man said, "What is to keep me from being baptized?" "Nothing," Philip said, "if you believe with all your heart." The man said, "I do. I believe that Jesus Christ is the Son of God." So the man stopped his carriage, and Philip baptized him.

When the man returned home to Africa, he had a lot to tell his queen and all the people of his country. Today there are still many Christians living in Ethiopia.

Something more to think about: How did Philip work for Jesus and His church? Why was it extra important that the man from Africa become a Christian? How did the man from Ethiopia get his faith in Jesus? What is still the way people become Christians?

Words to help us pray: Dear Father in heaven, we're glad that Your son Jesus, our Lord, is the Savior of the whole world and not just of one country or color. Send many more missionaries to those who do not yet know You and Your love. And make us willing to help in this work. In Jesus' name we ask it. Amen.

When a Man Named Saul Became a Christian

Because Stephen often spoke to people who did not believe the teachings of Jesus, he got into trouble with the leaders of the city, and they arrested him. During his trial Stephen said he saw Jesus standing at the right side of God in heaven. For saying that, they dragged him out of the city and killed him by throwing rocks at him.

Saul, a young member of the city council, watched the killing with pleasure. Saul had studied the Old Testament and was a very strict pharisee. He hated Jesus' followers. He believed that the Christians were teaching wrong things and that it was his duty to stop them.

So when Saul heard of people who believed in Jesus, he went to their houses and dragged them off to prison. He was so mean that many Christians moved to other cities. Then Saul decided to go after them wherever they were.

Saul was on his way to the city of Damascus when a light from the sky suddenly flashed on him. It was so bright and frightening that he fell to the ground. Then a voice said to him, "Saul, Saul, why are you trying to hurt Me?"

Shaking with fear, Saul asked, "Who are You, Lord?" The voice answered, "I am Jesus, the one you are fighting against. Now get up, Saul, and go into the city. There you will be told what you must do."

So Saul got up, but when he opened his eyes, he couldn't see anything. He was blind. His men had to lead him by the hand to Damascus. For 3 days he didn't eat or drink anything. But he did a lot of thinking and praying.

Finally God asked the Christian leader Ananias to go and visit Saul. At first Ananias was afraid to go. He knew Saul had come to arrest the believers in Jesus. But God said to Ananias, "Go. I have chosen him to serve Me. I want him to make My name known to Gentiles as well as to the people of Israel."

When Ananias came to Saul, he said, "Brother Saul, Jesus Himself appeared to you on the road as you were coming here. He sent me. He wants you to see again and be filled with the Holy Spirit." Then something that felt like fish scales fell from Saul's eyes, and he could see.

From that time on Saul was a changed man. He became a worker for Jesus and the best missionary Jesus and His church ever had. He started churches for Jesus all over the world.

Something more to think about: Why did Saul hate the believers in Jesus? What changed Saul from an enemy of Jesus to a worker for Jesus? Can you imagine what those first Christians thought and said when they heard that Saul was preaching and teaching for Jesus?

Words to help us pray:

> Lord Jesus, I have promised
> To serve You to the end.
> Oh, give me grace to follow You,
> My Savior and my Friend. Amen.